Mexican
Folk Tales

Mexican Folk Tales

Juliet Piggott

Illustrated by
John Spencer

CRANE RUSSAK, NEW YORK

American Edition 1976
Published by Crane, Russak & Company Inc.
347 Madison Avenue
New York, N. Y. 10017

ISBN 0-8448-0924-1

Library of Congress Catalogue Card Number 76-4165

PRINTED IN GREAT BRITAIN

Contents

The Story of
these Tales

IT HAS been said that a tale is a thing now existing only in a story, and that it is a thing of the past. And it is said too that a legend is a story, generally about a real place and often about real people, handed down the years by tradition. Legends are often thought to be historical, and sometimes they are. Myths can be described in various ways, but they concern natural or historical phenomena and are about supernatural people, their actions or events in their lives.

Some of the stories in this volume are legends and some are myths. But they are also all fairy or folk tales and they all belong to the past. And they all come from the country now known as Mexico.

Mexico is the stretch of land joining the United States of America to Central and South America, bounded by the Pacific Ocean on the west and the Gulf of Mexico on the east, and stretching south-east in a narrowing curve. It is a land of mountains; the Rio Grande extends along more than half of the northern border, and the great Sierra Madre is its double backbone, the ranges of which follow the coastal curves of the Pacific and the Gulf of Mexico.

It is also a land of deserts, where flowering cacti grow and scraggy mesquite trees and a shrub called huisache, which has tiny yellow round blossoms in the early summer. There are tropical forests too in the south-east. It is a colourful, varied land with a climate ranging from tropical through temperate to cool; a land of mountains, volcanoes, hills and lakes, of semi-arid country, lush fertile valleys and tropical coastal lowlands. It is a land of flowers and birds and butterflies.

It is also a land of maize or Indian corn. Many of the stories here concern maize, for it was the staple food of the early inhabitants of Mexico and has an important place in their mythology. Sometimes it is referred to simply as corn. And as in England the word in this sense means wheat and in Scotland oats, the word used here is an abbreviation of Indian corn and means the maize which has belonged to Mexico since the distant past.

And as the topography and climate of Mexico is and has been varied, so have been its inhabitants. It is generally thought that the American Indians came originally from Asia, by way of Alaska. The names of those old tribes and races of Indians echo still: Nahua, Toltec, Mixtec, Zapotec, Inca, Maya, Aztec. In the long centuries before the sixteenth century occupation of Mexico by the Spaniards the early development of the resources of the American continent had been in the hands of these ancient peoples. The Spaniards owed much to the Incas of Peru and the Aztecs of Mexico. Their way of showing it belongs to another page of history.

The history of Mexico also belongs to another place. But it was in 1520 that the Spaniard Cortez had finally conquered the ancient Aztec nation and destroyed the civilization which was theirs.

The capital was a fine city called Tenochtitlan. It is the capital of Mexico still, renamed Mexico City. It was on an

8

island in a lake in the long valley surrounded by mountains and known as the Valley of Mexico. Tenochtitlan had an aqueduct, and three causeways to the mainland. There were few roads but many canals. The houses were plastered white or washed a dark red with pumice. Montezuma II was the emperor when the Spaniards came. He ruled from a large palace set in a plaza surrounded by temples where the Aztec gods were worshipped and where sacrifices were made. There was a market place in the city where the Aztecs bartered for goods (although the cacao bean had a fixed value and so was an early form of money). And beyond the walls of the market place there were other temples and one of them had a door the shape of a serpent's mouth. It was here that the god Quetzalcoatl, the Plumed Serpent, was worshipped.

There was a belief that Quetzalcoatl had been a man, and a white one, and that he had come from across the sea in the east to rule. This belief had the important rider that he would return.

Quetzalcoatl belonged originally to the Toltecs and to certain Indian tribes before them. He was the god who first discovered corn. He was a part of the way of life in the Valley, or central plateau, of Mexico long before the Aztecs built Tenochtitlan and many, many years before the Spaniards, led by Cortez, arrived.

The Aztecs had gods other than Quetzalcoatl: Tlaloc the Rain God, to whom corn belongs because he stole it all soon after Quetzalcoatl found it, and Huitzilopochtli, who is the God of War and the Sun God as well, are but two.

Montezuma was aware of the discontent of the Indian tribes around Tenochtitlan, who greatly disliked their Aztec overlords, and he believed the prophecy that Quetzalcoatl would return in the year 1519 to reclaim his peoples and his lands. That was the year Cortez and his little army of only a few hundred men came to bring Christianity to the New World, to find treasure and to conquer. When Montezuma heard of their approach he believed the Spaniard was the deity Quetzalcoatl, the Plumed Serpent.

There were other strange reasons for the comparatively easy conquest of Aztec Mexico (where it is thought there were over four million warriors), and one of them was fear. Montezuma and the chief of the Texcocan tribe had argued about the prophesies of their respective soothsayers, and so certain was the Texcocan that his soothsayer's prediction that strangers would come and rule the land would come about that he wagered his whole territory against three turkey cocks as proof of his belief in the veracity of the prophesy. He and Montezuma played a ball game to decide the outcome of the wager. Montezuma lost. He was terrified that the Texcocan prophesy would come true and, because of the wager, believed it would.

There were strange happenings too, all of which added to the fear of Montezuma. Two temples were destroyed: one suddenly by fire and the other by lightning in a weird storm in which no thunder was heard. A comet was seen in day time. A ghostly woman's voice was heard calling to her children that they were lost.

And a strange bird was brought to Montezuma by hunters. It had a mirror in its head. Montezuma looked in it and saw the heavens reflected there. He looked in the mirror again and saw a group of armed men. He called for his soothsayers to explain the phenonomen of the mirror in the bird's head, but the bird flew away before they arrived and so they were unable to explain the reflections. It is not very difficult to imagine what their explanations might have been.

And then there were rumours coming into Tenochtitlan that monsters with four legs and human bodies protruding from their backs were approaching from the eastern coastline. These were the Spaniards on horseback, but the Indian tribesmen had not seen horses before and the stories of the approach of monstrous creatures were believed. The year was 1519, the year Quetzalcoatl was expected.

These unnerving events, prophesies and stories all led to the terror which was as powerful a reason for the swift success of the conquest as were the horses, cannon, muskets and steel swords (all previously unknown to the Aztecs) which the Spaniards used.

Inevitably the subsequent history of Mexico was less influenced by belief in an ancient god and the supernatural. Cortez and his army had destroyed the Aztec civilization by the year after it had been prophesied that Quetzalcoatl would come again from across the sea in the east to rule again. But the Aztecs remained. The Spanish and the Indian races mingled and there are now few Mexicans without indigenous ancestry.

And so it is that some of the stories here belong to the Indian tribes of ancient history and civilization, and some spring from the European culture and Christian tradition which the Spaniards brought from the east in the sixteenth century. The tales—legend or myth, whichever they are individually—all belong to the past, they all belong to Mexico, and they all belong to the people who lived there once and to the people who live there still.

Popocatepetl and Ixtlaccihuatl

BEFORE the Spaniards came to Mexico and marched on the Aztec capital of Tenochtitlan there were two volcanoes to the south-east of that city. The Spaniards destroyed much of Tenochtitlan and built another city in its place and called it Mexico City. It is known by that name still, and the pass through which the Spaniards came to the ancient Tenochtitlan is still there, as are the volcanoes on each side of that pass. Their names have not been changed. The one to the north is Ixtlaccihuatl and the one on the south of the pass is Popocatepetl. Both are snow capped and beautiful, Popocatepetl being the taller of the two. That name means Smoking Mountain. In Aztec days it gushed forth smoke and, on occasion, it does so still. It erupted too in Aztec days and has done so again since the Spaniards came. Ixtlaccihuatl means The White Woman, for its peak was, and still is, white.

Perhaps Ixtlaccihuatl and Popocatepetl were there in the highest part of the Valley of Mexico in the days when the earth was very young, in the days when the new people were just learning to eat and grow corn. The Aztecs claimed the volcanoes as their own, for they possessed a legend about them and their creation, and they believed that legend to be true.

There was once an Aztec Emperor in Tenochtitlan. He was

very powerful. Some thought he was wise as well, whilst others doubted his wisdom. He was both a ruler and a warrior and he kept at bay those tribes living in and beyond the mountains surrounding the Valley of Mexico, with its huge lake called Texcoco in which Tenochtitlan was built. His power was absolute and the splendour in which he lived was very great.

It is not known for how many years the Emperor ruled in Tenochtitlan, but it is known that he lived to a great age. However, it was not until he was in his middle years that his wife gave him an heir, a girl. The Emperor and Empress loved the princess very much and she was their only child. She was a dutiful daughter and learned all she could from her father about the art of ruling, for she knew that when he died she would reign in his stead in Tenochtitlan.

Her name was Ixtlaccihuatl. Her parents and her friends called her Ixtla. She had a pleasant disposition and, as a result, she had many friends. The great palace where she lived with the Emperor and Empress rang with their laughter when they came to the parties her parents gave for her. As well as being a delightful companion Ixtla was also very pretty, even beautiful.

Her childhood was happy and she was content enough when she became a young woman. But by then she was fully aware of the great responsibilities which would be hers when her father died and she became serious and studious and did not enjoy parties as much as she had done when younger.

Another reason for her being so serious was that she was in love. This in itself, was a joyous thing, but the Emperor forbad her to marry. He wanted her to reign and rule alone when he died, for he trusted no one, not even his wife, to rule as he did except his much loved only child, Ixtla. This was why there were some who doubted the wisdom of the Emperor for, by not allowing his heiress to marry, he showed a selfishness and shortsightedness towards his daughter and his empire which many considered was not truly wise. An emperor, they felt, who was not truly wise could not also be truly great. Or even truly powerful.

The man with whom Ixtla was in love was also in love with her. Had they been allowed to marry their state could have been doubly joyous. His name was Popocatepetl and Ixtla and his friends all called him Popo. He was a warrior in the service of the Emperor, tall and strong, with a capacity for gentleness, and very brave. He and Ixtla loved each other very much and while they were content and even happy when they were together, true joy was not theirs because the Emperor continued to insist that Ixtla should not be married when the time came for her to take on her father's responsibilities.

This unfortunate but moderately happy relationship between Ixtla and Popo continued for several years, the couple pleading with the Emperor at regular intervals and the Emperor remaining constantly adamant. Popo loved Ixtla no less for her father's stubborness and she loved him no less while she studied, as her father demanded she should do, the art of ruling in preparation for her reign.

When the Emperor became very old he also became ill. In his feebleness he channelled all his failing energies towards instructing Ixtla in statecraft, for he was no longer able to exercise that craft himself. So it was that his enemies, the tribes who lived in the mountains and beyond, realized that the great Emperor in Tenochtitlan was great no longer, for he was only teaching his daughter to rule and not ruling himself.

The tribesmen came nearer and nearer to Tenochtitlan

until the city was besieged. At last the Emperor realized himself that he was great no longer, that his power was nearly gone and that his domain was in dire peril.

Warrior though he long had been, he was now too old and too ill to lead his fighting men into battle. At last he understood that, unless his enemies were frustrated in their efforts to enter and lay waste to Tenochtitlan, not only would he no longer by Emperor but his daughter would never be Empress.

Instead of appointing one of his warriors to lead the rest into battle on his behalf, he offered a bribe to all of them. Perhaps it was that his wisdom, if wisdom he had, had forsaken him, or perhaps he acted from fear. Or perhaps he simply changed his mind. But the bribe he offered to whichever warrior succeeded in lifting the siege of Tenochtitlan and defeating the enemies in and around the Valley of Mexico was both the hand of his daughter and the equal right to reign and rule, with her, in Tenochtitlan. Furthermore, he decreed that directly he learned that his enemies had been defeated he would instantly cease to be Emperor himself. Ixtla would not have to wait until her father died to become Empress and, if her father should die of his illness or old age before his enemies were vanquished, he further decreed that he who overcame the surrounding enemies should marry the princess whether he, the Emperor, lived or not.

Ixtla was fearful when she heard of her father's bribe to his warriors, for the only one whom she had any wish to marry was Popo and she wanted to marry him, and only him, very much indeed.

The warriors, however, were glad when they heard of the decree: there was not one of them who would not have been glad to have the princess as his wife and they all relished the chance of becoming Emperor.

And so the warriors went to war at their ruler's behest, and each fought trebly hard for each was fighting not only for the safety of Tenochtitlan and the surrounding valley, but for the delightful bride and for the right to be the Emperor himself.

Even though the warriors fought with great skill and even though each one exhibited a courage he did not know he possessed, the war was a long one. The Emperor's enemies were firmly entrenched around Lake Texcoco and Tenochtitlan by the time the warriors were sent to war, and as battle followed battle the final outcome was uncertain.

The warriors took a variety of weapons with them; wooden clubs edged with sharp blades of obsidian, obsidian machets, javelins which they hurled at their enemies from troughed throwing boards, bows and arrows, slings and spears set with obsidian fragments, and lances, too. Many of them carried shields woven from wicker and covered in tough hide and most wore armour made of thick quilted cotton soaked in brine.

The war was long and fierce. Most of the warriors fought together and in unison, but some fought alone. As time went on natural leaders emerged and, of these, undoubtedly Popo was the best. Finally it was he, brandishing his club and shield, who led the great charge of running warriors across the valley, with their enemies fleeing before them to the safety of the coastal plains and jungles beyond the mountains.

The warriors acclaimed Popo as the man most responsible for the victory and, weary though they all were, they set off for Tenochtitlan to report to the Emperor and for Popo to claim Ixtla as his wife at last.

But a few of those warriors were jealous of Popo. Since they knew none of them could rightly claim the victory for himself (the decision among the Emperor's fighting men that Popo

16

was responsible for the victory had been unanimous), they wanted to spoil for him and for Ixtla the delights which the Emperor had promised.

These few men slipped away from the rest at night and made their way to Tenochtitlan ahead of all the others. They reached the capital two days later, having travelled without sleep all the way, and quickly let it be known that, although the Emperor's warriors had been successful against his enemies, the warrior Popo had been killed in battle.

It was a foolish and cruel lie which those warriors told their Emperor, and they told it for no reason other than that they were jealous of Popo.

When the Emperor heard this he demanded that Popo's body be brought to him so that he might arrange a fitting burial. He knew the man his daughter had loved would have died courageously. The jealous warriors looked at one another and said nothing. Then one of them told the Emperor that Popo had been killed on the edge of Lake Texcoco and that his body had fallen into the water and no man had been able to retrieve it. The Emperor was saddened to hear this.

After a little while he demanded to be told which of his warriors had been responsible for the victory but none of the fighting men before him dared claim the successful outcome of the war for himself, for each knew the others would refute him. So they were silent. This puzzled the Emperor and he decided to wait for the main body of his warriors to return and not to press the few who had brought the news of the victory and of Popo's death.

Then the Emperor sent for his wife and his daughter and told them their enemies had been overcome. The Empress was thoroughly excited and relieved at the news. Ixtla was only apprehensive. The Emperor, seeing her anxious face,

17

told her quickly that Popo was dead. He went on to say that the warrior's body had been lost in the waters of Lake Texcoco, and again it was as though his wisdom had left him, for he spoke at some length of his not yet being able to tell Ixtla who her husband would be and who would become Emperor when the main body of warriors returned to Tenochtitlan.

But Ixtla heard nothing of what he told her, only that her beloved Popo was dead. She went to her room and lay down. Her mother followed her and saw at once she was very ill. Witch doctors were sent for, but they could not help the princess, and neither could her parents. Her illness had no name, unless it was the illness of a broken heart. Princess Ixtlaccihuatl did not wish to live if Popocatapetl was dead, and so she died herself.

The day after her death Popo returned to Tenochtitlan with all the other surviving warriors. They went straight to the palace and, with much cheering, told the Emperor that his enemies had been routed and that Popo was the undoubted victor of the conflict.

The Emperor praised his warriors and pronounced Popo to be the new Emperor in his place. When the young man asked first to see Ixtla, begging that they should be married at once before being jointly proclaimed Emperor and Empress, the Emperor had to tell Popo of Ixtla's death, and how it had happened.

Popo spoke not a word.

He gestured the assembled warriors to follow him and together they sought out the few jealous men who had given the false news of his death to the Emperor. With the army of warriors watching, Popo killed each one of them in single combat with his obsidian studded club. No one tried to stop him.

That task accomplished Popo returned to the palace and, still without speaking and still wearing his stiff cotton armour, went to Ixtla's room. He gently lifted her body and carried it out of the palace and out of the city, and no one tried to stop him doing that either. All the warriors followed him in silence.

When he had walked some miles he gestured to them again and they built a huge pile of stones in the shape of a pyramid. They all worked together and they worked fast while Popo stood and watched, holding the body of the princess in his arms. By sunset the mighty edifice was finished. Popo climbed it alone, carrying Ixtla's corpse with him. There, at the very top, under a heap of stones, he buried the young woman he had loved so well and for so long, and who had died for the love of him.

20

That night Popo slept alone at the top of the pyramid by Ixtla's grave. In the morning he came down and spoke for the first time since the Emperor had told him the princess was dead. He told the warriors to build another pyramid, a little to the south-east of the one which held Ixtla's body and to build it higher than the other.

He told them too to tell the Emperor on his behalf that he, Popocatepetl, would never reign and rule in Tenochtitlan. He would keep watch over the grave of the Princess Ixtlacci-huatl for the rest of his life.

The messages to the Emperor were the last words Popo ever spoke. Well before the evening the second mighty pile of stones was built. Popo climbed it and stood at the top, taking a torch of resinous pine wood with him.

And when he reached the top he lit the torch and the warriors below saw the white smoke rise against the blue sky, and they watched as the sun began to set and the smoke turned pink and then a deep red, the colour of blood.

So Popocatepetl stood there, holding the torch in memory of Ixtlaccihuatl, for the rest of his days.

The snows came and, as the years went by, the pyramids of stone became high white capped mountains. Even now the one called Popocatepetl emits smoke in memory of the princess whose body lies in the mountain which bears her name.

The Fifth and Final Sun

BEFORE the sun which shines over Mexico and the rest of the world came into being, it is said that there were four previous suns. Each was destroyed in its turn until the present sun was created. There are, in Mexico, people who still refer to the sun which rises and sets, dividing day from night, year in and year out, as the Fifth and Final Sun.

There are many stories of the first four suns, and this is a part of some of them.

Each sun marked an epoch in the long, long saga of the creation of the world which is Mexico. Two gods were chiefly concerned with the four eras in the creation. One was Quetzalcoatl, who later found the corn with which to feed the new people the gods had created to populate the new world. He was a wise and benevolent god, and very powerful. His mother was a goddess, and his father also was a deity. Although greatly respected by the other gods, his parents were not venerated as much as he was.

Quetzalcoatl was tall and very strong. He had a broad forehead. One of the most distinctive things about him was that he had black hair, but his beard was fair, the colour of the corn of which, he was to become a patron.

He wore a hat made of ocelot fur and a quetzal bird was generally perched on his back. The quetzal bird is green. It lives in the mountains and is seldom seen. Its feet are strangely shaped, with two protruding toes. That very first quetzal bird of all used its toes to grip the god's shoulder in that long ago era when the gods were so occupied perfecting the world they had created.

Quetzalcoatl took his name from this beautiful jade coloured bird and from the ancient words, used first by the gods and then by men, meaning serpent and water. He was a great god and the waters of the earth, the earth itself and the winds in which the quetzal flew, all were under his control. Sometimes Quetzalcoatl is known as the Plumed Serpent, partly because of his name and partly because he could change his appearance and look like a feathered snake. But he did not do this very often.

The other god much concerned with the creation of the world but not, unlike Quetzalcoatl, greatly bothered by the welfare of its inhabitants, was Tezcatlipoca. He is known as the Black God because he was the god of night and its blackness. At the time of the first epoch it was as though Tezcatlipoca was the supreme god for there was no sun and the night and its blackness prevailed. The sky was lit only, and very faintly, by the Evening Star.

After the earth had been created it was an arid place and very dark. There were no tides, for there was no moon to regulate them, and there was no fresh water for there was no sun to draw the sea water up to the sky and transform it into rain.

The people who lived on the part of the earth which is now Mexico were not unlike the people who live there still, but they were very tall, with huge hands and feet and great big

23

eyes, which made it easier for them to see in the dark. In fact, the first human beings were really a race of giants. The giants built no houses and they planted no crops, for there were no crops to plant. Some say they lived on acorns and roots, but no one knows if this is true.

Tezcatlipoca and Quetzalcoatl were not friends. Quetzalcoatl became greatly angry with Tezcatlipoca because the Black God turned himself into a sun, for he tired of living in the dark sky. It was a dim sun and the giants called it the Smoky Mirror. It was the First Sun. Tezcatlipoca became that sun for selfish reasons, but all the same it was better for the giants to have a little light rather than no light at all. However, Quetzalcoatl felt it was not the task of the God of Blackness and Night to light the world, dim though the light was and much as it was needed. And so he challenged Tezcatlipoca to a duel.

Tezcatlipoca struggled hard, but he fell from the heavens into the ocean. The light of the Smoky Mirror went out in the water and the Black God might have drowned had he not turned himself into a tiger. In that form he was able to swim to land.

The giants who lived there had done nothing to irritate Tezcatlipoca, but he was filled with a great hunger and, since there was nothing else to eat which would satisfy the huge tiger, he ate most of them. They could not escape from him, for they could not see him coming.

Then Tezcatlipoca, having destroyed nearly all the first race of beings resembling men, returned to the heavens.

When his tiger fur had fully dried shining spots appeared on his coat and they can still be seen against the blackness of the night sky as the constellation of the Great Bear. It was many years after the tiger who is Tezcatlipoca took up his position in the sky that men thought his particular cluster of stars resembled a bear and not a tiger. But they had not heard the story of the duel between Tezcatlipoca and Quetzalcoatl.

The return to the sky by the Black God, in the form of a tiger, ended the epoch of the First Sun.

The earth remained poorly lit by the spots on Tezcatlipoca's fur and the Evening Star, but after a while Quetzalcoatl turned himself into a sun. He felt that the earth needed light very badly if it was not always to remain a dreary and arid place. He shone more brightly than Tezcatlipoca had done as the Smoky Mirror, with the result that Tezcatlipoca became jealous. But he did not challenge the sun to a duel.

At night, while Quetzalcoatl rested, dimming the light which was his, the spots on Tezcatlipoca's coat could be seen as he lay in the sky. But by day, when the sun was shining, he was invisible. One day at high noon, when the sun was at its brightest, Tezcatlipoca suddenly reached out his great tiger claw and snatched Quetzalcoatl from the heavens and tossed him into the sea. Quetzalcoatl could not see Tezcatlipoca coming towards him and he could do nothing to defend himself. As he splashed down into the ocean the earth became dark again.

But more than that happened, since one of Quetzalcoatl's duties was the regular movement of the winds. As he fell from the sky he lost control of them and a great hurricane, the like of which had never happened before or since, swept around the face of the earth as Quetzalcoatl fell. The great hurricane uprooted the few growing things on the land, leaving the few giants who remained there very little to eat. The hurricane died down once the sun had fallen into the sea and the land was dark again, but the damage was done. The giants nearly starved. In order to stay alive they became smaller and smaller

and in this way they needed less and less food. Eventually they turned into monkeys. And so the earth's population of giants gradually disappeared and their place was taken by a race of monkeys, and the era of the Second Sun was truly over.

There were a great many other gods in the heavens apart from Quetzalcoatl and Tezcatlipoca. These gods decided that as both of them had been failures as suns they would not allow either of them the privilege of lighting the world again. And so, Tlaloc, the god who controls the rain and the fire from the heavens, was turned into the new sun.

Tlaloc was a minor god compared with Quetzalcoatl and Tezcatlipoca and his duties as Rain God had been minimal since without a sun shining constantly upon the land and sea there was scarcely any rain to control. Quetzalcoatl had greater powers than Tlaloc, even though Tlaloc had become the sun. Quetzalcoatl decided to show his strength.

Tlaloc had power over the fire from the heavens but Quetzalcoatl could use forces of devastation too: he suddenly began hurling down upon the earth meteors and great flashes of lightning, and he caused the mountains to erupt. Much of the earth was covered with molten lava springing up from the newly created volcanoes and the air became steamy from the boiling waters of the geysers which Quetzalcoatl opened up. Fire and rocks cascaded from the skies. Sulphur fumes also made it impossible for the few monkeys who had managed to evade the fire and lava and boiling water to breathe. So it was that the surviving inhabitants of the world became birds and flew high above the world to safety, partly carried from the dangers below by the winds, both strong and gentle, which Quetzalcoatl blew for them.

And the light Tlaloc gave was put out by the holocaust and the earth became dark again, and that was the end of the era of the Third Sun. It lasted a very short time, so quickly did Quetzalcoatl loose the forces under his command.

The Fourth Sun was a transformed goddess. The gods thought that by selecting a goddess the wrath and jealousy of the gods would not be invoked and that the new sun would therefore be a permanent one. The chosen goddess was very beautiful and always wore a green skirt the colour of jade. As the sun, she lighted and heated the world for, it is said, three hundred and twelve years. This was much longer than Tlaloc had lit the world, but it was a short era compared with the total time it took to establish a lasting sun.

She was one of the water goddesses, but while she was the sun she concentrated entirely on creating conditions on the land which would be suitable for human beings. So, during those three hundred and twelve years the gods not only caused the birds to return to the earth and to fly among the trees, but they created another type of creature—men and women.

In the three hundred and thirteenth year of the era of the Fourth Sun, the era of the creation of mankind, Tezcatlipoca taunted the beautiful goddess one night while she was resting from her duties of being the sun. He teased her and said she burned so brightly during the day in order to prevent the gods from approaching her and not because she was dutifully fulfilling her functions of warming and lighting the earth. In her frustration at this false accusation she wept and, in her fury at what Tezcatlipoca had said, she lost control of the waters of which she was a goddess, in the same way as Quetzalcoatl had lost control of the winds of which he was god when Tezcatlipoca had tossed him into the sea. The goddess' tears put out her light and then cascaded down upon the earth which was swallowed up by the mighty flood. This destruction was all the fault of Tezcatlipoca. The goddess of the green skirt had been the most diligent of all the suns so far.

It is not known whether Tezcatlipoca meant his behaviour towards the lovely goddess in her jade green skirt to have the result of flooding the earth or not, but devastate the world with her tears he did. There are some who say the entire human race was drowned except for one man, and some say all the men and women, except for one man, became fish. Certainly there had been no fish until the light of the Fourth Sun was put out by the weeping of the goddess.

Quetzalcoatl tried to lift the earth from under the waters of tears, but it was heavy even for him, with all his great and godly strength. Perhaps from shame for the weeping of the goddess in the jade green skirt and the subsequent havoc he had caused, Tezcatlipoca helped him. Together the two gods heaved the earth upwards and the waters fell away from it and they fastened it securely in the sky. But still there was darkness. The era of the Fourth Sun was over.

All the gods, and there was a great multitude of them, then went to the greatest of their cities, Teotihuacan, and consulted together. They decided it was essential to have a permanent sun to light the earth by day. They also decided there must be a permanent moon to give illumination by night, for they considered the Black God, Tezcatlipoca, was too powerful during the night which was his, with only the Evening Star snd the spots on his tiger coat to shine during the hours of blackness when the sun rested.

For four days the gods discussed the matter, sometimes arguing and sometimes in agreement, as to who should become the Fifth Sun. As the eras of the first four suns had all ended in disaster the gods realized among themselves that, on this occasion, it would have to be a sacrifice on the part of whichever god became the new sun, rather than an honour conferred upon him or her. Only in this way could the Fifth Sun become the final one.

Two gods offered to sacrifice themselves in order to give light to the world. One was rich and strong and the other was poor and feeble. The rich and strong god thought by sacrificing himself he would become richer and stronger. The poor and feeble god only wanted to light and warm the earth.

At the end of the fourth day the gods, Quetzalcoatl and Tezcatlipoca among them, agreed to allow these two gods to each try and become the sun. A mighty fire was built in Teotihuacan. Coals and logs of wood were cast upon it and so great was its light that all the heavens were illuminated. Then the deities commanded the rich and strong god to leap into the great fire and sacrifice himself. But he feared the flames and the heat and he hesitated. Three times he drew near to the fire as though to jump in, and three times he drew back.

Then the poor and feeble god approached the conflagration and stood looking at it for a little while. Suddenly he gave a great cry and leapt into the centre of the fire. A vast flame sprang upwards, and across the earth, like a huge arrow of fire in the sky. Then it faded and, where the tip of the flame had touched the sky, the sun appeared, shining brightly as it has done ever since and always moving onwards in the direction the arrow of flame had taken.

A mighty roar of delight rose up from Teotihuacan. Quetzalcoatl and all the gods, even Tezcatlipoca, were well satisfied with the Fifth Sun. They knew it was also the Final Sun.

One god, however, was displeased. He was the rich, strong god who had offered to sacrifice himself but had failed to do so. Through his own cowardice the great power of being the sun was not to be his. In his jealousy and shame he flung himself into the fire.

But the flames were dying and the embers had lost their great heat. No vast arrow of flame came springing forth. But slowly, from the ashes, the moon appeared and sailed slowly up into the sky in feeble pursuit of the sun.

The gods were angry at the way the moon had been created. One of them picked up the nearest object he could find, which happened to be a rabbit, and flung it by the leg at the moon as it started its endless chase after the sun. It was a good aim. The marks the rabbit's body made on the surface of the moon are there still, and can be seen when the moon is full. The moon with its rabbit markings is still pursuing and never catching up with the sun's journey of light and warmth around the earth, in this present era of the Fifth and Final Sun.

How Jiculi Served His Tribe

HE lay on his side and tried to move. The cords, magically spun from the fibres of the Mexican Soap Plant and the Giant Mexican Lily, cut into his arms and legs. He relaxed again to ease the pain. He could think of no way of escape: even if he could squeeze his way out of the tough fibres binding him he would not be able to crawl out of the cage which imprisoned him, for it was made out of closely woven branches of the sharp and spikey Parsley Leaved Thorn interlaced with thongs of deerskin. Only with the sharpest of knives could he free himself and his obsidian bladed hunting knife had been taken from him and thrown into the undergrowth. He desperately needed help. But from where would, or could, it come?

He could think of no way to relieve the biting pain of the fibre cords (the witches had bound him very tightly) and, to take his mind off his acute discomfort, he began to reflect on how he had come to be in this painful and seemingly hopeless predicament.

It was Jiculi, Prince of the Huichol tribe, who lay prisoner there. He was a young man, endowed with wisdom, modesty and practicality beyond his years. He lived among his people on the Pacific west coast of Mexico, in the northern mountains of the area known today as Jalisco.

Maize was the main crop of the Huichol and Jiculi did much to help them with its cultivation. As well as giving advice as to the best time to plant the seed and to cut the heavy heads of maize, he was not too proud to work in the fields with his tribe in the valley where they lived. Jiculi and his people were at peace and contented.

This was not pleasing to the evil forces who roamed and stalked the forests and mountains around the Huichol valley. These mysterious and malevolent powers resented the respect in which the prince was held by his tribe.

It was, perhaps, inevitable that the time would come when these evil beings should decide to prove their power over the good Jiculi and that they should do it first by hurting the tribe he both loved and served.

A group of witches was given the task of poisoning the entire maize crop. In the early evening they concocted a noxious brew and each witch filled a gourd with the liquid. When it was dark they scattered and flitted away to the Huichol maize fields, the witches dipping their hands into their gourds and flicking the poison so that one drop fell on each plant. They did their work silently in the moonlight as Jiculi and his people slept the sound sleep of peaceful men.

But in the morning the effect of the witches' activities was quickly discovered: the tall stems of maize were blackened, the leaves had become a sickly ochre and the heads, which had been so nearly ripe, drooped, their tassels and sheaths dark brown and the grain inside soft and pappy.

Jiculi was told that the whole crop was ruined and famine faced the entire Huichol tribe. Long before the sun had reached its noon-day position, Jiculi had run from field to

33

field and seen for himself the devastation. He, with his people, knew that magical and malicious powers had been at work but only he, wise man and mentor that he was, knew how to counteract the magic.

He charged each man, woman and child, all who could walk and had the strength to carry even the smallest pot of water, to gather by the river, bringing with them all the containers they possessed. The whole tribe, save only the sick, the crippled and the very, very young, soon grouped by the river bank with a great assortment of vessels, ranging from gourds to deerskin water bags.

Then, under Jiculi's direction, they set about making a series of human chains from the river to all the maize fields. Quickly the gourds and pots and leather containers were filled with clear river water and passed along, emptied and then handed back again to the river bank. Jiculi ran from

group to group, encouraging the weary and helping the frail, telling his people all the while that each maize plant must be watered before noon. For the rest of the morning the Huichol people worked as they had never worked before, pausing neither for rest nor refreshment.

By midday the task was done. Each diseased maize plant still looked bedraggled and discoloured, but each had been freshly watered—and before the sun had reached its zenith.

Jiculi then told his people to do no more work for the rest of the day but to go home and eat and sleep. There were some who grumbled for they could not understand how, by merely watering their crop at speed, they could have saved its yield but they were few who spoke thus. The Huichol people had faith in their prince and knew he would not have driven them to so much work in the space of one short morning for no purpose.

Their faith was justified indeed.

When dawn broke the following morning the maize was all restored. It was as though the magical poisonous blight had never been. The plants looked healthier and the cobs more bountiful than they had done before they had been touched by the evil.

The Huichol rejoiced greatly, and loudly praised their prince. But he found their repeated thanks tedious and told them to go and tend their fields as usual while he went into the forest to hunt for game. As always, they obeyed him and the sounds of their ecstatic expressions of delight at the salvation of their harvest faded as Jiculi picked up his wooden knife with its sharp blade of obsidian and made his way out of the valley towards the mountains.

The evil ones up there knew that Jiculi and the good he stood for had triumphed over their malice. This they could not tolerate. The magic poison of the witches had been overcome and the evil ones swore that their magical powers, against the Huichol and their prince, would be invincible from that day on.

There were many beings and creatures in those high Jalisco hills, devoted to the cause of malevolence, but there was only one sorcerer. He cannot be described for he had no constant shape or form. Sometimes he would be a great boulder, sometimes a gnarled and ancient tree. He could become any beast of his choice or even take on human form. He could speak with the voice of the viper or a whisper as beguiling as the wind. He could speak the languages spoken by men and in the tongue of the Huichol he was very fluent.

The evil beings summoned the witches to a giant rock face overlooking the forests above the maize fields and in a crashing voice of thunder the rock face spoke to them. They knew they were in the presence of the Sorcerer.

He told them the manner by which the benevolence of Jiculi was to be overcome by the powers of evil. The plan was to turn Jiculi into a snake and then set him among his people so that they would kill him and, in so doing, would themselves destroy their own prince and the good he did for them.

Firstly Jiculi had to be captured. The witches were told to make a cage. They wafted through the forest to where the Parsley Leaved Thorn grew thickly. No man could pass through the thickets of Thorn, so sharp and entangled were its tough and wiry branches, each covered with sharp spikes. The witches were impervious to its clutches and they gathered a bundle with which to build a cage big enough to hold a man. Swiftly they glided through the forest and up the mountain and, below the rock face, which was the Sorcerer, they constructed the prison for Jiculi. From the fibres of the Mexican

Soap Plant and the Giant Mexican Lily which had suddenly appeared, fully grown, at the behest of the evil ones, they swiftly produced sisal cords with which to bind him. The bars of the cage they fastened with strips of deerskin which the Sorcerer conjured for them and from the heap of unused deerskin a large and handsome deer sprang to life.

Then the Sorcerer spoke to it in the language of deer and instructed it to go through the forest to where the evil ones knew Jiculi was hunting alone.

The witches flitted and glided through the trees as Jiculi stalked the deer which had suddenly appeared before him. It led him through the forest higher and higher up the mountain, to the bottom of the rock face, the witches wafting and weaving through the trees in silent pursuit of their quarry. Suddenly the deer vanished.

Jiculi moved swiftly to examine the heap of deerskin thongs in the place where he had last seen his prey, but before he reached the spot the witches crowded in upon him. Shrieking and jabbering, they trussed him up with their fibre cords and thrust him into the thorn cage.

This was how Jiculi came to be in his predicament high up in the mountains—alone.

The witches had vanished and, certainly, would have been of no help. The Huichol did not know where to look for him: indeed they had not missed him. It was not unusual for him to go out on solitary hunting expeditions and he had told them he was going on this one.

The Sorcerer remained silent. Jiculi continued lying on his side. There was nothing else he could do. He was fearful, hopeless and abandoned.

Then he saw an amazing sight. Standing outside the cage was a lion. But it was no ordinary lion. It had no fur, but was

covered instead with feathers. Long whispy feathers formed the mane and sleek flat feathers covered the rest of its body. The lion was plumed in a rainbow of colours. The waving plumage of its mane ranged from deep blue through shades of turquoise and green to a brilliant yellow and the rest of the body was a shimmering scarlet, flecked with white, orange and purple spotted feathers. It was both beautiful and dreadful, and Jiculi was afraid of it.

Suddenly he no longer felt the tight cords binding his arms and wrists. He glanced at them and saw they had disappeared or magically melted away. Even as he thankfully stretched out his swollen arms he realized that the fantastic plumed lion could be none other than the Sorcerer, and he was more fearful.

But the Sorcerer in his splendid disguise did not reveal his identity himself. Instead, with the mouth and tongue of a lion, he spoke gently in the Huichol tongue. He softly urged Jiculi to pluck one of the feathers from his mane, telling him that by doing so he would secure his release.

"I, the Plumed Lion of Many Hues, caused my minions to make the fibre cords which bound your arms and hands to vanish. You must now pull whichever plume you choose from my fine headdress and once you have it in your hand all your bindings and the cage in which you lie will vanish also."

But Jiculi was wise and his fear of the cage and of the creature which was the Sorcerer did not dim his instinctive discernment. He shook his head.

Again the Plumed Lion tried to beguile him into plucking a

feather. It lay down very close to the cage, pushing its mane through the thorny branches. Here was magic indeed: not one thorn snared the brilliant coloured feathers. The temptation to take one was great: the Plumed Lion moved its head and a jade green feather tickled Jiculi's face.

Intuitively the young prince knew that if he did as the Plumed Lion bid, release from captivity would not be his, but another and more fearsome torment. What his fate would have been Jiculi never knew, but doubtless the feather would have turned him into a snake as plotted by the evil ones.

The Plumed Lion lost patience and disappeared. Instantly the fibre bindings reappeared and cut into Jiculi's arms more harshly than before. The Sorcerer had resumed his guise of a great rock face, and silence returned to the mountain.

Although the powers and forces of evil considered they reigned supreme in the Jalisco highlands, this was not so. There were gods there too and of them the God of Maize was the greatest. These gods had watched Jiculi's care for the Huichol tribe and had noted with pleasure, particularly the Maize God, how he had saved the crop from the poisonous havoc of the witches. They had been saddened by the punishment the evil ones had given Jiculi and proud of the way he had resisted the temptation of the feathered lion.

The time had come to help Jiculi.

All the birds were commanded to summon the mice of the forest. Flying in groups over Jalisco they warbled and sang and twittered to the mice, calling them to the thorny cage.

Scampering and running came the mice, in hundreds and thousands, to obey the summons. They circled the cage and, while the great company of birds watched from the trees and boulders, gently they began to nibble the deerskin thongs binding the thorny bars. They scampered all over and around the cage, chewing, gnawing and biting the tough branches until Jiculi lay on a soft heap of sawdust. Finally, gently and without touching Jiculi at all, they bit through the sisal fibres binding him. The birds all joined together in a chorus of thankfulness as the mice scurried away into the undergrowth, their task completed.

Jiculi slowly stretched and rubbed his bruised and bleeding limbs. He rested a while on the soft pile of sawdust the mice had made. He was very stiff and his legs and arms were cramped and smarting, but he was just able to stand and stagger for a few steps and then, as his circulation returned, he raised his arms in a salute of thanks to the birds and the vanished mice and set off at a slow trot for the valley and his tribe.

At last the evil ones realized their plans had been thwarted. In his voice of thunder the Sorcerer called for the witches and told them to recapture Jiculi. Shrieking and yelling they flew through the forest and, finding only a pile of sawdust and chewed up thongs where the cage had been, they at once made for the Huichol valley after Jiculi.

He heard their weird shoutings and tried to run, but his legs were still too painful for him to be able to move with any speed.

Once again the gods came to Jiculi's aid. Just as the witches were almost upon him for the second time, the gods contrived to turn the Huichol prince into a splendid young stag with fine spreading antlers. As once he had been a prince among men, so now he appeared as a prince among deer and, with the longest and most slender legs, he could run faster than any other deer in the whole of Jalisco.

Jiculi bounded away from the witches with a supernatural speed and their cries of anguished rage faded in the distance.

The powers of evil, swearing not to be outwitted by the powers of good, transformed the witches into a pack of hunting hounds. And, just as the prince could run faster than any other deer, so each witch-hound could outrun the swiftest of ordinary hounds.

The race was on: leaping and galloping through the forest and around the valley, swimming and splashing across the river and back again and then into the forest once more the chase continued, the hounds baying and slobbering as they tore after their victim. Imperceptibly at first and then increasingly, the witch-dogs of the evil ones began to gain on Jiculi.

The gods appreciated that it was not only safety which Jiculi craved, but the ability to serve his Huichol people again. And so it was that the gods gave, through Jiculi, a special and perpetual gift to that tribe.

Suddenly, in a forest glade, the splendid stag stopped. The baying of the hounds came closer and closer, but the creature stood immobile. Slowly it sank into the ground as though through quicksand. Its antlers were disappearing when the hounds reached the glade and their frustrated howls of anger reached the ears of the evil ones who knew they had been overcome finally in their fight against Jiculi, Prince of the Huichol.

Where the stag had disappeared there appeared, buried in the ground, the gift of the gods to the Huichol tribe. The gods had turned the stag, not back into its human form, but into the first peyote cactus plant.

Even the God of Maize concurred with this unique creation, for the knowledge of the cultivation of maize had already been given by Jiculi to his people.

When their prince did not return to the valley the Huichol

tribe sent out search parties. For many days they mourned and sought Jiculi. Finally, when it seemed they would never find him the gods caused one of these groups of men to pass the place where Jiculi, in the form of a stag, had sunk into the ground. And there the peyote was discovered, buried in the loamy soil of the forest.

The gods also caused the Huichol people to try eating it when the first cactus had been taken back to the valley. The tribe no longer had their prince but they had peyote. They soon learned of its wonderful powers of healing and found, too, that peyote brings luck and longevity. It can even give the gift to couples, both young and not so young, of falling in love.

And so peyote has been precious to the Huichol since the days when the gods and the forces of evil fought their battle of magic in the mountainous forests of Jalisco. It has been prized and venerated since those events in ancient times when Jiculi became a stag and then the first peyote. The gods used the young prince to overcome the forces of the evil ones and in doing so they allowed him evermore to serve his tribe, not as he had done before, but in the special form of a cactus with magical power.

The Golden Man and the Finger Men

AFTER the gods had created the world, with its mountains and plains, rivers and lakes and seas, with fish to swim in them and with macaws and quetzal and other birds to perch and nest in the trees, they decided their earth was too bountiful for only fish and birds. There was room for creatures other than those which flew above the earth and those which swam in the rivers and lakes and seas.

So they made insects. And they made snakes and lizards and caterpillars. After that butterflies and moths were made. The lizards ate insects and the caterpillars ate leaves and butterflies drank from the flowers, as did the bees which the gods had also made. Still there was more than enough food on the earth for all these creatures.

So then the gods made animals: mice and rabbits and tigers and ocelots and dogs, and they made coyote too. More and more animals they made, and more reptiles as well and many more different kinds of birds and fish and insects, and there was enough food to sustain them all, and more beside.

The gods were very pleased with all they had created and the birds, the fish, the reptiles, the insects and the animals were content with the life they had been given on the earth and in its rivers and lakes and seas.

But there was something missing in the world and for many aeons of time the gods did not know what it was. The gods were unhappy because they knew there was something lacking in the world they had made and they knew, too, that there was something also lacking in the heavens.

At last they realized what was missing. The earth was beautiful to look at and bountiful to live in: and yet all the different creatures they had made who lived upon it, enjoying its produce, never told the gods they admired the glories of the plains and mountains, the cacti and the mesquite trees, the orchids and the poinsettias, nor did they ever thank the gods for their own creation or the means of their survival. They did not do this for they could not speak. The world was a silent place: the only sounds were those of the winds and the waves and the moving waters of the waterfalls and rivers.

And so the gods at last learned that the thing which was missing in the heavens was praise and thanks from the creatures of the world below and that which was missing in the world was a race of beings capable of speech.

Thus it was that the gods decided to make a whole new creation of creatures to live off the bounty of the earth and the waters on and around it, and able to fill the heavens with their praises for all they saw around them.

Having agreed to make a new race of creatures, the gods had to decide how to do it: the new race of beings would be very different from those already existing and the gods realized that they would have to use new and different methods in their creation.

First of all, the gods wanted to make it possible for the birds and the animals and other creatures to communicate

47

with one another. Only by learning how to do this would the gods be able to make the new beings, not yet created, capable of filling the heavens with the sound of their praise.

So the gods gave the creatures upon the earth the gift of communication. And the creatures used this gift among themselves, but they gave no praises to their great benefactors, the gods. The earth and the heavens echoed with the sound of roaring and squeaking and whistling and barking and chirping and grunting. The world was no longer inhabited by silent creatures, but the gods did not understand their noises. They knew that if the heavens were ever to resound with praises from the earth the gift of communication was not enough. The gift of language must be given to the new beings. The gods did not like the sounds the birds and animals made and agreed that the gift of language would be given to the new beings only.

The gods discussed this important matter of giving the gift of language to the new beings, and they decided that in order for them to be able to use it they must be able to stand upright and that their heads must be at the top of their bodies and not in front of them. Hands and arms these new creatures would have, and only two legs, and they would not be covered with fur or thick hide or feathers, for with their hands they would make coverings of their own choosing for their bodies. And the gods then decided that another special gift must be given to the new creatures as well as those of life and language: they would be given the gift of reason.

After many consultations the gods agreed upon the appearance of the new beings they were now ready to make. But they could not agree on the material they should use. Some suggested they should use plaited grasses, and others thought that stitching leaves together would be the best way to make the new beings. And others thought they should be carved from sandstone and yet some wanted to chip the beings from the hardest rocks.

At last they decided that clay would be the best material to use. The gods gathered mud from the river bank and made it into a great pile. When it had dried a little they each took a piece and began moulding it into the shape they had agreed upon.

Each of the gods modelled the clay in the manner pre-scribed, and yet each of the clay figures was different from the others. They all had heads and necks, two eyes, a nose and a mouth with teeth and a tongue inside it, and ears the shape of shells. Each clay figure had two arms and four fingers and one thumb attached to the extremity of the hands protruding from their arms, and they all had two legs, with feet attached and five toes pointing in the same direction as the figure's nose on the face at the top of the model. And yet, when each of the gods had finished making their clay figures they were all surprised at the variety of new creatures they had made. Some figures were much bigger than others, and some had rounder bodies than the rest. The modelling of the faces, the cheeks, the noses and mouths and chins and the shape of the eyes and eyebrows varied the most. Not one single figure was identical to another: each god had made a unique, yet similar, clay model.

Each and every one of the company of gods was well pleased with their individual creations, as well as the whole race of new creatures they had all made together. But the gods were cautious. Before bestowing upon the clay figures the gifts of life and of language and of reason they wanted to test them to ensure their bodies were as durable as the bodies of the birds and the fishes and the insects and the animals and

49

reptiles they had made before.

The new creatures were already proven to be as tough as the birds and other living things apart from fishes, for they did not crumble and wither to dust in the air. So the gods agreed the new creatures should be submitted first to the test of water.

Each god lifted up the clay model he had made, and all the new creatures were thrown into the river from the banks of which the mud from which they had been made had been taken.

There was a mighty splash.

Even as the spray fell back into the river the gods saw their new creatures had not survived the test: they had all melted and the river was filled with churning mud. In silence the gods watched the current take the remains of their latest creation away to the sea.

Then they let out an anguished wail of sorrow.

But their despair did not last for long, so eager were they for the heavens to resound with their praises and the world to be filled with the new beings they had envisaged. So, with no argument and little discussion, they decided to carve the new beings from wood, following the same design as they had used for the clay models.

Again each god carved a single figure, and each one had a head with a face upon it, a neck, two arms and hands and fingers and thumbs, an upright body and two legs, with feet and toes attached. And again, while each puppet resembled the others each was different from the rest. Some were big and some were small and the faces of the wooden figures were fixed in a multitude of expressions.

As in the case of the birds and insects and animals their bodies could and did withstand air. The gods again put their

new creatures to the test of water. They threw the puppets into the river and again there was a mighty splash.

As the spray died down a cry of delight rose from the gods: the wooden puppets floated and bobbed in the river and the gods cheered as it carried them down to the sea. Their new creatures could withstand water, even as could the fishes and the other creatures of the rivers and the lakes and the sea.

The gods were very pleased indeed with the new beings they had made, but they wanted them to live on the earth and not in water. So they picked them out of the sea, each god carrying the puppet he had carved, and set them down by the river bank.

Again the gods showed caution. They agreed that before giving their new creatures the gifts of life and of language and of reason the puppets should be submitted to a final test. So confident were the gods that they had made a race of utterly superior beings that they decided to put them to the great test which neither bird, fish, insect, animal nor reptile could survive: the test of fire.

The gods built a huge pile of grasses and leaves and dried cactus plants and set it alight. And when it was burning fiercely they threw the puppets they had made into the flames.

A cloud of smoke rose up and quickly was blown away. The gods saw that their new creatures had turned to ashes. In silence the gods waited until the ashes cooled and the remains of the wooden puppets were just a heap of grey dust.

The grief of the gods was great indeed.

But they were still determined to populate the world with a new race of creatures which would fill the heavens with praises, creatures the shape of the clay models and the wooden puppets, for they knew that that was a good shape. And they conferred together and agreed that their next creation must be able to withstand the great test of fire, for they thought only in this way would the new beings be proved to be superior to all the other living creatures in the world.

Some gods considered the new creatures should be chipped from rock crystal and others wanted to use obsidian, and yet others wanted to use jade or turquoise. A few gods wanted to use copper. After a long period of time spent in argument and discussion about the merits of the materials most likely to withstand the great test of fire, the gods agreed that the new creatures should be made of gold.

The gods then scattered and spent many days gathering nuggets of gold, and when each found enough to fill a kerchief they all gathered by the river bank. They discovered they had not got enough gold nuggets for each to make a new creature of gold and so together the gods fashioned one single figure out of all the gold they had found. Some gods made the head, and others the body, and yet others the limbs and the hands and thumbs and fingers and the feet and the toes. One god fashioned the nose of the new creature and one made its eyes and another its ears and yet another its mouth, and others its tongue and its teeth.

And when the golden statue was finished the gods were well pleased with their handiwork: it was a beautiful new creature that they had made. And it did not crumble and wither in the air.

So they put it to the test of water and the gold did not dissolve. The gods pulled the statue from the river and as the drops of water fell from it the sun shone upon it and the statue sparkled, shining brightly and reflecting the sunlight and they thought it more beautiful than ever.

Then the gods built a mighty fire and threw their golden statue into it, and it withstood the heat and the flames, and

53

after the flames had died down and the smoke had blown away and they saw their new creature standing in the ashes it seemed to them to be even more beautiful than before. It was as though the fire had polished it and the gold of which it was made shone more brightly than even it had done when it was wet.

The time had come to give their new creature the gifts of life and of language and of reason. In unison the gods breathed upon the golden statue and it became alive, and it was the first man.

The Golden Man spoke, but there was no one to answer him. The gods made no reply. His reason told him he was the only human being in the world. This grieved him greatly and instead of the heavens being filled with the thanks and praises of the new man for the gifts he had been given they were filled with the sounds of his weeping and his words were not the words of gratitude. He called out abuse and insult at the gods for giving him a body of gold and with it the knowledge of riches, and for giving him no companions other than birds and fish and insects and animals to whom riches would be of no use. He had been given the knowledge of the riches of the earth and he had no companions, not one, with whom he could share this knowledge. The Golden Man was a creature of ingratitude. Not one word of praise to the gods for the earth and its beauties and all their other creations passed his lips.

And the displeasure of the gods was total.

Their new creation was beautiful and rich in a way that no other creature upon the earth was rich and yet, for all the gifts they had bestowed upon him he was as indifferent and ungrateful to his creators as the gold from which he had been made.

The gods despaired. The heavens were filled with the

sounds of their wailing as well as the insults of the Golden Man which rose up from the earth.

One of the gods was so anguished by the behaviour of the Golden Man that his hands shook, and he dropped his obsidian bladed machet. As it fell its sharp cutting edge severed the fingers from his left hand. He let out a cry of pain. In his mortification he screamed out that his fingers should become the new creatures he and the other gods had tried so hard to create.

And the gods who had exhausted the best of their materials with which to make the new creatures echoed his despairing command that the new beings should be formed from the severed fingers of the god, and they echoed that they should be the same shape as the Golden Man and the wooden puppets and the clay models before him.

So it was that as the four fingers fell from the heavens and appeared in the world they took on the form of the Golden Man, and they were made of flesh and blood and bones, and they had hearts within them.

The gods did not submit the new creatures, the Finger Men, to the tests of water and of fire. Such tests had been proved to be useless when all the gods had really sought for were praises for the gifts of creation to fill the heavens. So they just breathed upon the Finger Men in unison and gave them, in one last attempt to obtain that which they so wanted, the attributes of life and of language and of reason. The hearts of the Finger Men began to beat and they were alive and they could speak and they could think.

The Finger Men moved about the earth and they spoke with one another and they thought about all they saw and touched, and they marvelled at its beauty.

Not very long after the Finger Men had been given the

gifts of life and of language and of reason they met the Golden Man. They spoke to him, but his replies were harsh. They touched him and his hands were cold. They thought about him and while they could not fully understand him they knew him to be very rich and to have the knowledge of increasing wealth. And their reason also told them his heart was very hard.

The Finger Men did not, at that early stage, know what or how to eat. But drink they could do, and they went to the river and carried water in their cupped hands and gave it to the Golden Man. He drank it and as he thanked them, the first words of thanks he had spoken in his short life, his heart softened. The Finger Men, with the river water, had done that which the gods had not thought of doing, giving the Golden Man a tender and not a rigid heart made only of solid gold.

Then the Golden Man and the Finger Men moved together about the earth, the Golden Man showing the Finger Men the riches as well as the beauties of the world and he showed them, too, how to increase the riches and still marvel at the beauties. And they all spoke with one another and they exclaimed delightedly at the wonders they saw and with their reason they rejoiced in the knowledge the Golden Man shared with the Finger Men.

Suddenly the heavens were filled with thanks and with praises and, at once and at last, the gods were truly satisfied.

They ordained that from then on there would be rich men and poor men on the earth and that each in their different ways would help the others as they moved about the earth, and that they would all fill the heavens with their praises and that those praises would be the music of the gods.

And the Golden Man and the Finger Men thus became the new people, whose descendants live in Mexico still.

The gods were now content with their new race of creatures. And it was only a little while after the heavens first rang with praises and with thanks that the great god Quetzalcoatl discovered how the new people should be fed and the gift of life kept strong within them.

But in the short time before he did that the heavens were ringing with the praises and thanks of the new people, for the Golden Man and the Finger Men had only had the gift of life for a little while and did not yet know what hunger was. And for that brief period in the aeons of time when the gods made the world and the living creatures upon it and before the first rich man and the first poor men knew they were hungry they were well satisfied with each other and their creators. And in that little space of time the gods were satisfied with their own, the new people.

The Rabbit and the Two Coyote

A COYOTE, a Mexican or North American prairie wolf, was walking through the forest one night. He had already eaten a rabbit that evening and he was not hungry. He had had a good sleep after his meal and so he was not tired either. He was just walking and feeling rather bored. His brother had also eaten a rabbit, but after their meal the two coyote had separated, this one to his favourite place in the forest.

After a little while he came to a clearing among the trees and there, in the middle of the open space was the pool he liked so much. Around three-quarters of the pool the banks were smooth and grassy, but one quarter was different. There were boulders of rock lying there and the bank was steeper, and there was also a tall pillar of rock sticking up like a finger, pointing to the sky above the towering trees. And so, not because he was really thirsty, but because he had nothing else to do, he went to the stony bank of the pool and, under the pillar of rock, had a long drink.

In the starlight he sat by the pool, resting on a slab of stone, watching the ripples from the place where he had drunk

58

spread out across the water, growing further and further apart until there were no more and the surface of the pool was still again.

Because he was still bored he continued to sit there. Presently the moon appeared from behind a cloud and its round pale yellow reflection shone up at the coyote from the depths of the pool and the coyote wondered about the orb which had appeared in the water.

There was a thumping sound behind him and, as the coyote turned round to see what the noise was, a rabbit appeared beside him.

The coyote was much surprised, for rabbits usually ran away from him, and his brother too, scurrying to the safety of their burrows. It was most unusual for a rabbit to approach a coyote. But this was a very remarkable rabbit. He was also the brother of the two rabbits the coyote brothers had eaten that evening.

The coyote spoke first. "What brings you here, to this forest pool, so late at night? Are you thirsty, perhaps?"

"No, I am not thirsty."

"Can it be you are hungry then? There are some young and tender reeds over there. Have you come to eat them for your supper?"

"I am a little hungry, but I have eaten enough green matter and I do not hunger for reeds, however young and tender. I think I would like to nibble a piece of cheese."

"I too am very fond of cheese. But I know rabbits do not often eat it. How very strange. You are surely a most remarkable rabbit."

"Yes," said the rabbit, "I am."

And that was the only truthful statement the rabbit made to the coyote.

Having made his truthful utterance the rabbit proceeded to drink from the pool.

"You said you were not thirsty, and yet you drink. I find you strange. Are you not afraid of me?"

"No, Why should I be?"

"Because I have already eaten one rabbit tonight and, for all you know, I may very well want to eat you. In fact, I think I shall want to eat a rabbit again—very soon."

The rabbit did not answer. He took another long drink instead.

Then he jumped back and squatted beside the coyote again on the stone slab.

"I appreciate your telling me," he said, "that you might want to eat another rabbit very soon. As a matter of fact I already knew you had eaten one this evening. And I can assure you that you do not really even contemplate eating me, in spite of what you say."

The coyote was annoyed. He was not hungry and yet it seemed foolish to sit talking with a rabbit which would make a most excellent meal. And so he said to the creature which he planned to eat later: "You have satisfied the thirst you told me you did not have, and I have already drunk. And it would seem that you are only hungry for cheese, and I am not yet ready for my next meal. Shall we sleep for a little while and then resume our most interesting conversation?"

"That is a very good idea. Let us sit closer to the pool. I might get thirsty again before I fall asleep."

The coyote thought this remark odd, but agreed. They moved forward a little. The rabbit showed no fear and the coyote was confident he would be an easy victim when he began to feel in need of his next meal.

They sat there together in silence, each perched on the edge of the smooth stone under the pillar of rock. And then the coyote closed his eyes.

He was nearly asleep when the rabbit suddenly began thumping the ground and talking excitedly.

"Wake up, wake up! I have most excellent news for you."

The coyote again felt irritated. "What news can you possibly give me which will please me? I was about to go to sleep and you have thoroughly woken me up."

"Cheese," said the rabbit.

"Cheese! What are you talking about? There is no cheese here in the forest."

"Yes, yes! Look! There in the pool."

And the coyote looked into the still black water and saw again the reflection of the moon at the bottom of it.

"I wondered about that. I was looking at it before you came and joined me here. Is it really a cheese?"

"Indeed it is. See how round it is. And pale yellow. It must be just ripe and ready for eating."

"I believe you are right. We must get it out."

"If we drank all the water in the pool it would be a simple matter to get at the cheese," said the rabbit.

"Foolish creature. We could never drink the whole pool. No, we must dive in and get it that way."

"Very well, I shall go," said the rabbit, moving away from the coyote along the pool's bank.

But the coyote did not trust the rabbit. He said such odd things and his whole manner was so strange. In fact, the coyote thought the rabbit might get the cheese and swim with it across the pool and run away, taking it with him into the forest. And if that happened he would lose not one meal, but two.

So he called out and said, "Don't you go diving in. I shall do that. You are two small to lift that great round cheese from the bottom of the pool. Come back, and stand here and I shall pass the cheese to you when I have fetched it."

The rabbit looked at the coyote for a moment and then bounded back to him.

"You are very kind," he said. "Thank you. I think it really would be easier for you to get the cheese."

And then the rabbit suddenly gave the coyote a push, and he fell into the water. He came up to the surface spluttering, and swam round and round in a circle. "What did you do that for? I was going to jump in myself, on top of the cheese."

"I only wanted to help," replied the rabbit. "Do not waste your energy swimming in circles like that. Dive down and fetch the cheese."

"But I cannot see it any more," called the coyote, sounding half sad and half cross. "My eyes are full of water and the ripples I made when you pushed me in have hidden the cheese."

"Well, try," said the rabbit firmly.

And the coyote did try, several times, to reach the bottom of the pool. But he got tired and had to swim to the bank, where the rabbit helped him out on to the boulders under the finger of rock.

"I promise not to push you in again, and I really was only trying to help."

The coyote was panting so much he could not reply. So the rabbit went on: "Let us wait until the pool is still again and we can see where the cheese is. Then you can jump on top of it as you meant to do before."

When the coyote had got his breath back and they could see the reflection of the moon clearly, undisturbed by any ripples, he said thoughtfully: "I am beginning to wonder if I can dive as deep as that. I could not touch the bottom once when I tried just now."

"Nonsense," said the rabbit cheerfully, "of course you can. I have seen that you are a very good swimmer. And you are big and strong, unlike me, and clever too. I am only remarkable."

The coyote was flattered and said he was willing to try again.

"I think it might help," said the rabbit as the coyote stood on the stone ledge under the pillar of rock looking down at the yellow orb in the smooth water, ready to jump on top of it, "if you took a heavy stone with you."

"Why?" asked the coyote, turning away from the pool and looking at the rabbit.

"Because, although I know you can dive to the bottom of the pool once you are in the water, I think a heavy stone would take you there more quickly. And," he added, "I want some of the cheese just as much as you do. Furthermore, I want it soon."

So the coyote, anxious to get the task of fetching the cheese over, agreed. The coyote stayed on the ledge, looking greedily into the water while the rabbit found a piece of rock which he said would be just right; heavy, but not so heavy that the coyote would not be able to carry it, together with the cheese, to the surface again.

Then the rabbit pulled a creeper from a tree and tied the rock to the coyote's neck.

"Your legs must be free for swimming and you will use your mouth to pick up the cheese," said the rabbit before the coyote could make any comment.

The rabbit tied the rock to the coyote in such a way that the boulder rested on the ledge and the coyote did not know how heavy it was.

"Now I shall jump in."

"Yes, you do that," said the rabbit, giving him a violent push from behind.

The coyote would not have been able to jump into the pool by himself, so heavy was the rock tied to him, and the rabbit did not mind at all pushing him even though he had promised he would not. After all, he had only spoken the truth to the coyote once since he had joined him under the pillar of rock. And once, the remarkable rabbit considered, was quite enough.

The coyote said nothing as he fell into the water, so surprised was he at being pushed. His mouth filled with water as the rock sank rapidly to the bottom of the pool, dragging the helpless coyote with it.

When the ripples had died away and the water was smooth

again the rabbit peered down into the pool. He could not see the body of the coyote in the blackness, only the reflection of the moon, round and yellow, and, thought the rabbit, not really looking like a cheese at all.

He bounded back through the forest, his mind on the next revenge he wanted to take. He had got rid of the coyote who had killed and eaten one of his brothers. Now he would get rid of the coyote who had had his second brother as a meal. The rabbit did not know the coyote were brothers themselves. And if he had known he would not have considered it important for, to him, it most certainly was not that.

On his way back to his burrow and when he was not far from it, but quite a long way from the forest with the pool in which the moon was reflected and in which the dead coyote lay, the rabbit passed by an onion patch. It was not very big, but it had a great many onions in it, and the rabbit could smell that they were ripe. He jumped over the ditch surrounding the patch and saw, for dawn was breaking by this time, that the onions were large and succulent.

He ate half of them and most excellent they were.

Then, his hunger gone and the fields and valleys around him filled with sunlight, he bounded the little way to his burrow where he fell asleep.

The owner of the onion patch and his wife were very distressed by the loss of half their onion crop. The man said that he would watch for the rabbit that night in case it came back. But the woman knew her husband would only fall asleep and she said she would take care of their remaining onions. As the owner of the patch was lazy and glad not to have to try and stay awake all night he allowed the woman to do whatever she might to guard the remaining onions.

The woman made an image of a rabbit out of wax and put it

right in the middle of the onion patch. Then she and her husband went into their house for, by then, noon had passed and it was time for their siesta.

The rabbit did not feel the heat of the sun, deep in his burrow, and came out in the afternoon, partly because he was hungry again and partly to look for the coyote who had killed his second brother.

He went straight to the onion patch where he knew there was succulent food waiting for him. But when he arrived he did not immediately start eating, delicious though the smell of the onions was. He saw the wax model of a rabbit standing in the middle of the patch and he wondered who this stranger might be. The only way to find out thought this truly remarkable rabbit was to ask. So he bounded up to the waxen image and said. "Who are you?"

There was no reply.

The rabbit spoke again. "What do you want in this onion patch from which I have recently begun taking my meals?"

Silence was the only answer.

The rabbit hopped round the model and then realized it had no life and therefore couldn't speak. He was angry at having temporarily lost his dignity by speaking to a lifeless object. He decided to knock the image of the rabbit down and, moving away from it first, bounded back towards it and jumped heavily upon it, landing with his four feet pressed upon its back. The wax model indeed toppled over but so did the rabbit, for his feet were firmly imbedded in the wax.

The rabbit had to lie on his side trapped in a most un-dignified position, in the heat of the sun. The rabbit was very angry indeed. In fact, he was remarkably angry. But, for the time being, he was powerless to escape.

After two hours had passed the owner of the onion patch

came to see whether by chance his remaining onions had been eaten in daylight and, to his delight, he found they had not. His delight was even greater when he saw how his wife had trapped the thieving rabbit. He called her to bring a cauldron of water, and he quickly built a fire. He and his wife then set the water to boil for they proposed putting the rabbit and the wax model into the hot water, thereby cooking the rabbit and, at the same time, melting the wax in which it was trapped.

The rabbit was appalled when he realized what the humans were doing. But good fortune was with him. The couple went back to their house to wait there until the water boiled, for the afternoon sun was very strong and it was cooler indoors.

They had only just gone when a coyote appeared in the onion patch. He smelled the trapped rabbit. He was hungry.

The rabbit recognised the coyote as being the one who had eaten his second brother. The coyote did not know that his brother was dead, having been killed by the trickery of the very rabbit he now planned to eat. Perhaps if he had known he would not have been so easily tricked himself.

The rabbit greeted the coyote politely and the coyote returned the greeting equally politely.

And then: "Please will you help me get my feet out of this wax?"

"Why should I do that?"

"Because the human beings, a man and a woman, put that cauldron of water to boil in order to boil chickens for me to eat. Stuck in this wax as I am, I shall not be able to enjoy them. Of course, if you help me I shall share the chickens with you."

The coyote thought it strange that the rabbit should want to eat even one chicken, but the thought of a whole meal of fowls, ready boiled, was tempting.

"I did not know rabbits liked boiled chicken," he said.

"I am a very remarkable rabbit," was the reply. "Now get me out of this wax."

"Very well, I shall help you in return for at least half of the chickens." And he pulled each leg of the rabbit free from the wax.

"Thank you," said the rabbit. "Now I shall go and tell the man and the woman I am ready for the chickens. You sit here by the cauldron and call me if the water boils before I come back."

So the coyote sat down to wait and the rabbit ran off. He did not run in the direction of the house belonging to the owner of the onion patch and his wife, but the coyote did not know that. Instead the rabbit went back to his burrow to wait for the outcome of his trickery.

Soon the man and his wife returned to the onion patch. They were amazed to see a coyote sitting quietly by the cauldron, watching the water as it slowly came to the boil. They were even more amazed to see that the rabbit had escaped from the wax model. Since coyote usually eat rabbits the couple were furious that this one had evidently helped the rabbit which had eaten half their onion crop to get away. And it infuriated them still further to see the coyote just sitting there, as though it was proud of what it had done.

With a sudden movement the man bent down and tipped the cauldron of now boiling water over the coyote. The animal jumped quickly, but not quickly enough. His tail was badly scalded and he ran howling towards the forest.

The rabbit was lying at the entrance of his burrow and, hearing the cries of the coyote, he bounded off after them.

The rabbit thought of the pool and the tall pillar of rock where he had tricked the other coyote to death and as he followed along he made a new plan of revenge. He guessed the coyote was making for the pool, so he took a short cut through the forest and hurried along at his fastest pace, his hunger completely forgotten.

The coyote did indeed go to the pool. His scalded tail was still hurting and, without looking round, he jumped into the cool water to ease the pain. He swam round for a little while and when he felt better he climbed up the rocky bank, and shook himself dry.

Only then did he see the rabbit leaning against the pillar of rock. He had no idea that the body of his brother was lying at the bottom of the pool and that the rabbit was responsible for its being there. But all the same, he was angry with the rabbit.

"Why did you leave me sitting by the cauldron of water? The humans, the man and the woman, brought no chickens. They scalded my tail and it is all your fault."

"Indeed it was not my fault. How was I to know the cauldron would be upset? For all I know you tipped the cauldron yourself."

"I most certainly did nothing of the sort. The man tried to pour all the water over me. If I had not been so agile I might have been scalded to death."

"I am sorry about your tail," said the rabbit.

"Never mind about that. It is better now. Chickens, you said. I saw none. Not one."

"The chickens were not ready. I know that. I went and looked. If they had been ready the humans and I would have brought them out and boiled them and then I would have shared them with you. I told you all that before."

"Yes, you did and that is why I pulled your legs out of the wax. But you should not have left me alone like that. Where are the chickens? Are they ready now?"

69

"I should think they must be."

"If they are not I shall eat you," said the coyote, wondering why he had been foolish enough not to eat the rabbit at once instead of entering a conversation with him again.

"Better to have a meal of several chickens than just one rabbit," said the rabbit, guessing the coyote's thoughts "And anyway, my last meal consisted of half the onions in that onion patch where we met before. I do not think you would enjoy me for I would surely taste very strongly of onion."

"With that I do not agree. But where are the chickens?"

"The man and the woman have them. They are getting them ready for me, I mean us, to eat."

"Will they bring them here or do we have to fetch them?"

"We must fetch them, of course. How can the human beings know where we are?"

"Very well, let us go."

"I am afraid you must go by yourself," said the rabbit.

"Go by myself! Certainly not. The man and the woman would only throw more boiling water over me."

"Yes, perhaps they would. I shall go by myself and then you will be quite safe."

"That is equally ridiculous. I do not trust you to bring the chickens back to me. We must go together."

"We cannot do that. One of us must stay here."

"Why?"

"Because, and I really cannot think why you have to ask, if we both go the sky will fall down."

"The sky fall down? Why should it?"

"This pillar of rock, which I am propping up, supports the sky and unless one of us leans against it it will topple over. And if that happens the sky will crash to the ground. It is very simple, really."

"But the pillar has never had to be propped up before. I have been here many times, my brother too, and I know."

"I did not know you had a brother," said the rabbit. "Where is he?"

"I do not know. We separated after our last meal. I rather expected to find him here."

"What did you eat for your meal?"

"A rabbit each," replied the coyote.

"Oh," said the rabbit. And he looked into the depths of the pool, but could see nothing except the sun's rays sparkling on the water.

"I shall eat you for my next meal unless you come with me to fetch the chickens."

"But what about the sky falling down? If that happened we should never find them."

"I still do not understand why the pillar of rock has never had to be propped up before."

"Oh, you do ask obvious questions. Because it has only just become loose."

"In that case I shall prop it up while you go and fetch the chickens. If you do not come back by dusk I shall come and find you and then I shall eat you."

"Even if the sky falls down?"

"Yes, even if that happens. But it will not happen."

"And why not?" asked the rabbit.

"Because my brother comes to the pool most evenings and when he comes . . ."

"If he comes," interrupted the rabbit.

"When he comes," continued the coyote, "he will prop up the pillar of rock for me while I find and eat you."

"That is excellent," said the rabbit. "How pleasant to have so reliable a brother."

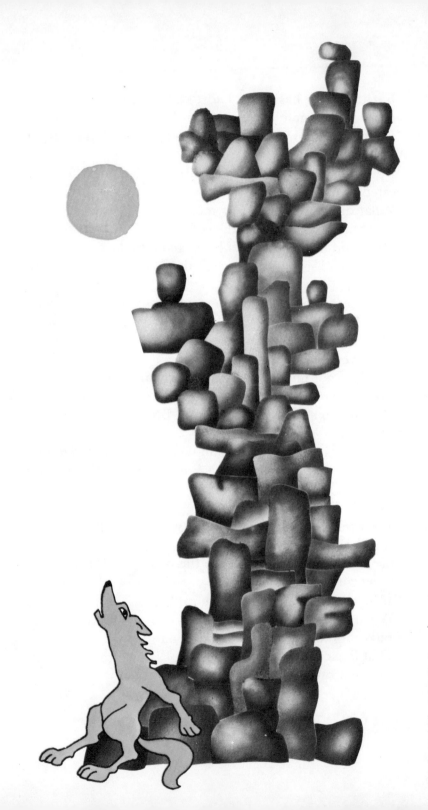

"Have you got a reliable brother too?" asked the coyote.

"No," said the rabbit. "I have no brothers."

"Oh, how remarkable."

"Yes. I am a remarkable rabbit. Now, let us change places. I shall go and get the chickens."

"Yes, you do that. And remember, if you do not bring them back either I shall come and eat you or the sky will fall down."

"I shall bring them back. I do not forget I promised to share them with you in return for freeing me from that wax."

"Much good that has done me so far," said the coyote. "Go now and come back quickly."

They changed places. The coyote leaned against the pillar of rock and listened until the sound of the rabbit's scudding feet died away in the distance.

The pillar of rock against which he was leaning did not feel loose, but he did not dare move in case the sky fell down.

The rabbit ran straight to the onion patch where he ate all the remaining onions, then went into his burrow and fell asleep. It had been a very full day, and a very satisfactory one.

The coyote fell asleep too. It was dark and he was unable to stay awake any longer, waiting for either the rabbit to return with the chickens or his brother to arrive to hold up the sky for him. He stirred in his sleep, losing his balance, and toppled into the water. And there, in the moonlit pool, he drowned as his brother had done the night before.

A Story of a Flood

Long, long before the Spaniards crossed the Atlantic Ocean and came to Mexico there was a great flood there. It covered the whole country, the plains, the deserts, the forests and even the mountains. The people were all drowned and, if it had not been for one member of the Huichol tribe, there would have been no people in Mexico at all, not until the Spaniards came centuries later.

It happened this way.

There was a hard working man of the Huichol tribe. He was not very old and not very young and he toiled most of each day tending his little field in order to raise enough maize for his needs. He had no wife and lived entirely alone in hermit fashion in a cave. His only companion was his dog, a small black bitch.

The time came when he decided he should find a companion from his tribe and raise a family. But first he needed to grow more maize: his field only yielded sufficient food for himself. So he began clearing a part of the forest adjoining his small plot.

Every day he felled at least three trees but every day they grew again. No matter how hard and long he worked, his labours had no effect and he was unable to enlarge his maize field.

He was in despair. It seemed to him that the Earth Goddess who had caused his maize to grow so well was thwarting him in his efforts to grow more and this he could not understand. He cried out to her and begged her to explain.

Suddenly she appeared to him, a thing she had done for no man before.

She took the form of a little old woman, bent with age but sprightly, with thick long hair the colour of earth and eyes the colour of ripe maize. She wore a tunic the colour of sand and she leaned on a staff made from a branch of sprouting mesquite wood.

The Earth Goddess pointed with her staff to the north, to the south, to the west and to the east. And then she pointed it to the sky and then to the ground. The salate trees which the Huichol had chopped down that day immediately stood up again, and the Goddess began to speak.

"My bones, which are as old as time, tell me a great flood is coming. This staff of mesquite wood is sprouting and this too means much water is on the way. I made the soil fertile in the desert where the mesquite tree grows and only moisture is needed to turn it into fields for maize, for beans and for pumpkins. The flood will be of benefit, but not until the whole earth is submerged and all the Huichol tribe and all the creatures and the plants that grow in the ground are drowned."

The man was greatly afraid, and even when the Goddess told him that he alone among all his tribe had been chosen to survive, he was still afraid.

"How can I survive if the earth is to be covered with water and all that lives in it and upon it are to be swept away into the Great Darkness by the flood?"

The Earth Goddess told him to have courage and patience and to do exactly as she said. Pointing with her sprouting staff at the large salate tree under which they stood, she told him to cut it down.

"I will not raise it up as I did the other trees you felled:

75

this one is for a most special purpose." And she went on to tell him in great detail what else he must do to survive the flood. "It will come at the end of the fifth day and, unless you do as I have instructed you, the Earth of which I am Goddess will be barren for evermore and the Huichol people will never walk upon it again."

And then the little old woman who was a goddess vanished.

The Huichol chopped down the tree with the sharp obsidian-bladed hatchet he always used. He hacked off the branches and from the trunk he fashioned a box, a little longer and a little wider than himself. Then he made a lid to fit it so exactly that not a chink of light could get in. Into the box he put five grains of maize, five beans and five small pumpkins as the Earth Goddess had commanded him to do. He chose the smallest pumpkins he could find and they were very young and tender. The fully grown ones were too bulky to fit in the box.

On the morning of the fifth day the Earth Goddess appeared again and told the man to get into the box and to call his dog and make it get in too. The man was pleased to hear this: he had feared the little creature would be drowned in the flood and his awe of the Earth Goddess was such that he had not dared plead for its life when she had told him that he alone would survive the coming waters.

He lay down in the box with the little black bitch in his arms and the sprightly old woman who was a goddess picked up the heavy lid, as though it was no heavier than a leaf, and pressed it into position. The man had made the box well and he could assure the goddess, when she asked him, that he could see no light at all. There was not even the tiniest of cracks in the wooden container in which he lay.

The sky became overcast as noon approached, but this the

man did not know, for he was in total darkness. A few hours after he had climbed into the wooden container, however, he heard the steady beat of raindrops on the lid above him, and then a creak and a sensation of pressure which he guessed was the Earth Goddess sitting on the box. And so she was. He could not know it, but she had a macaw perched on her shoulder.

It was a quaint sight: the little old woman, in her sand coloured tunic, her yellow eyes flashing and her earth coloured hair, sodden with rain, straggling down her back. On her shoulder the brightly hued macaw of yellow and blue, stretched its wings trying to shake off the falling rain. But soon it gave up trying to keep its feathers dry and crept under the thick mane of the Earth Goddess' hair and, tucking its head under its wing, fell asleep.

The rain fell in steady silver rods sounding a ceaseless tattoo on the lid of the wooden box. The tempo increased and after a while the man became aware of a swaying sensation. His wooden refuge was afloat. He now knew for certain he would not drown and the relief, together with the gentle rocking motion of the rising flood water and the sound of the beating rain all combined to lull him into a very deep sleep. And his dog slept too.

He was asleep for five years. During the first year the box with its cargo of one Huichol, one black bitch and five grains of maize, five beans and five little pumpkins drifted over the land towards the north. The next year it floated back to the south. During the third year the box moved west across the waters and then, for another year, its slowly sailed east. All the while the rain came steadily down.

The waters covering the earth were deeper than any Huichol could measure, but there was no one to take any

soundings for the only person to escape the flood slept in his floating wooden box.

Only the Earth Goddess was awake as she drifted above her flooded domain. Day by day, she sat there calmly watching the rising waters with her yellow eyes and stroking the sleeping macaw.

During the fifth year the box did not drift but floated becalmed in one position on the ever rising water.

Suddenly the rain stopped.

The Earth Goddess's tunic and hair dried quickly in the sun and she lifted the macaw out from under her hair. It ruffled its blue and yellow feathers as they dried but still did not wake.

As the fifth year drew to its end the level of the waters began to subside and, before many days passed, the box landed gently on the top of a tall mountain.

The Earth Goddess took the macaw off her shoulder and held it high above her. It awoke and opened its curved beak, letting out a loud screech. This woke the man and the dog. The dog began to bark and the man tapped on the lid of his little dark prison. Quickly the old woman sprang off the box and opened the lid with one hand, the macaw perching on the other. The dog leapt into sunshine. The man stretched and rubbed his eyes and clambered out on to the mountain. The macaw, which until then he had never seen, flew from the Earth Goddess' hand and settled on his shoulder. And the man and the black bitch and the coloured bird looked at the flood waters surrounding the mountain, and to the man it seemed as though he were standing on an island in an ocean reaching to the horizon in every direction.

He took the five grains of maize and the five beans and the five small pumpkins from the box and tucked them into his tunic. The little dog snuffed the Earth Goddess' hand and she stroked its head. The macaw flew to the ground and began making little furrows with its hooked beak.

From this moment the great volume of water retreated rapidly.

The Earth Goddess pointed with her sprouting staff of mesquite wood to the north, to the south, to the west and to the east, and then to the sky and then to the ground. As the man, the dog and the macaw watched, the deep ocean fell away from the mountain in a mighty waterfall and the land appeared below. Forests sprang up again with incredible speed and the macaw suddenly flew away and disappeared among the new and leafy trees, its screech echoing above the silent land.

The man turned to the Earth Goddess but she was gone. She had vanished like the flood waters and the man never saw her or the macaw again.

But a breeze blew gently up from the valley and it carried her voice to him. "Enlarge your field as you were doing before the great rainfall and plant the maize and the beans and the pumpkins and perhaps a wife will come to you from where I am now speaking, behind the wind."

He made his way down the mountain, the black bitch trotting behind him, and came to the cave where he had lived before his encounter with the Goddess of the Earth. He put the five grains of maize, the five beans and the five small pumpkins in three separate heaps on the ground inside the cave, picked up his machet and went to the edge of the forest adjoining his field.

And so again he began cutting down trees in order to enlarge his field so that he might grow enough maize to support a wife should the Earth Goddess send him one, as she had half promised.

The trees he cut down did not spring up again as they had done before the Earth Goddess had appeared to him and saved him from the flood. But he was slow in beginning his work for he realized, even as he started on his task, that it was all of no use: all the Huichol except himself had been lost in the great waters and belonged now to the land of the Great Darkness and he would never find a wife by himself and never raise a family. Many times he wondered if he had heard the words of the Earth Goddess correctly when they came to him on the mountain, and whether it was worthwhile enlarging his field.

After a few days of dreary tree cutting he noticed for the first time that the tortillas for his evening meal had been prepared for him on his return. He had been too dispirited to notice before that he had not made them himself. He ate the tortillas. They were doughy inside, crisp outside and very good.

He resolved to return to the cave early the next evening and see by whom his meal was cooked. The Earth Goddess in her guise of a little old woman perhaps? She was the nearest to a human being he had seen since his long sleep in the floating box. He decided to ask her if she really would send him a wife from the place from which she had spoken behind the wind, and tell her he would not enlarge his field and plant the beans and the pumpkins and the maize unless she would give him that promise.

On the following day he hid himself, late in the afternoon, in the undergrowth near the entrance of the cave and, to his amazement, saw his dog take off its skin as though it was a tunic. As it did so the creature turned into a woman with black hair and black eyes, bright and shining. She was not very young but she was not even close to being old.

The man kept absolutely still as he watched the woman take kernels of maize from a natural basin shaped indentation of rock filled with water in the wall of the cave. She placed the moist mixture on a large concave stone lying flat on the earthen floor and, using a piece of smooth stone, a little larger than her hand, she ground it to a thick paste. The wet coarse flour she then placed in three flat portions, one on each of the three stones of the hearth at the entrance of the cave.

The man crept forward and snatched up the black dog skin and threw it into the fire. And in silence he and the woman watched it burn, and did not look at one another.

He poked the black haired pelt with a stick until it was only a heap of grey ash. The woman whimpered a little, saying her skin felt sore. But he knew instinctively what to do and took some more soaking maize from the filled rock trough and he soothed her body with it.

Then she smiled at him and bade him eat two of the tortillas which were by then toasted on the three-stoned hearth. She ate the third herself and spoke to him of the maize and the beans and the pumpkins they would plant and eat together in the future.

"They, like us, came from the wooden box in which the Earth Goddess saved us," she said.

"But you also came from behind the wind."

"That is true. I did."

The children and their descendants of the man and the woman, who had been a black bitch, repopulated the Huichol tribe, and so it was, long, long afterwards, when caves were no longer used for homes and houses were built instead, that the Spaniards came to Mexico.

The Beastly Creature and the Magical Flower

THERE was a man who was a widower. But he had three daughters and, as they grew up, while they did not take the place of their dead mother in the household they did look after their father very well indeed. They cooked for him and they cleaned the house for him and they sewed for him. And, most important of all, they gave him much affection. It can be said that they cherished their father; and it can equally be said that he cherished them. It was a flower which was responsible for one of the daughters leaving home. A single flower.

The father of the three girls (and they were young women for the youngest was sixteen and the middle sister was eighteen and the eldest had just turned twenty) used to leave them alone in their country home once a month, or sometimes once in two months. This was because he was a merchant and he had to go to the city or sometimes to the seaport, to attend to his business. And every time he returned from one of these excursions (which he always made on horseback, for it was long after the Spaniards first came to Mexico bringing horses with them) he would given each of his daughters the present for which she had asked. Sometimes when he asked them what they wanted him to bring back they would suggest a new dress each. And sometimes it would be a comb or length of lace which they wanted, or a bangle or a necklace.

Just before the merchant set off on one of his trips he enquired of his daughters, as he always did, what they would like him to bring back for them from the city. And the eldest asked for a new dress, a red one this time.

"Very well, my dear, you shall have it. I shall choose for you the brightest and most beautiful shade of red I can find."

He turned to the middle daughter and smiled at her, and she said: "Please, Father, may I have a new dress too, and may it be a yellow one?"

He said he would find for her in the city a dress of the brightest and most beautiful yellow.

And then he said to his youngest daughter: "Tell me, my littlest one, what colour would you like your new dress to be?"

To his surprise, and that of her sisters, the youngest member of the family said she did not want her father to bring her back a dress at all, but that she would like him to pick a single flower for her and bring her only that.

"What kind of flower? There will be many to choose from as I ride home from the city, and why should I not pick a whole bunch of flowers for you, my youngest child?"

But the girl said she really only wanted one flower and that she left the choice to her father. "You will see a flower and know it is the one which will please me most."

"How shall I know? There are a multitude of flowers in bloom now. How shall I possibly be able to tell which particular blossom will be truly pleasing to you?"

"I cannot explain to you how you will know, but you will."

And with that her father had to be content.

The elder daughters thought their sister was foolish to ask for a flower instead of a pretty new dress, but they did not tease her about it for she was a gentle girl and very sensitive. They thought she had probably asked for a single flower in order to save her father money, even though thrift to him was neither necessary nor, indeed, his inclination where his three daughters were concerned.

The youngest of the three young women of the household did not again mention the flower she knew their father would pick for her and, for fear of hurting her feelings, the others did not talk excitedly about their new dresses while their father was away. Usually they would all chatter together about the presents their father would bring them and speculate about the occasions on which they would wear their new finery. And so the three sisters busied themselves about the house, not talking very much and the youngest of them the most silent, mending such clothes of her father's as needed mending and preparing for his return.

The merchant finished his business in the city within a few days. Then he spent a whole morning looking for a red dress for his eldest daughter. He finally selected one of the purest scarlet. It was as bright as a flame and very beautiful.

In the afternoon he began his search for the yellow dress his second daughter wanted. It was late before he found the dress he liked better than any of the others he had seen. It was a pure rich yellow with not a trace of red or orange in it and was as bright as a yellow flame is bright. It, too, was very beautiful.

The following morning the merchant carefully packed the two dresses in his saddlebags, mounted his horse and set off for home.

When he had previously made such trips to the city, he started on his return journey very early in the morning, as soon as it was light, and ridden at speed before the heat of the sun forced him to slow his horse's pace. But on this occasion he had not packed overnight and it took him some time to fold the red dress and the yellow dress in such a way that they would not get greatly crumpled in his saddlebags. And, apart from the late start, he could not ride quickly for he was looking at the flowers by the wayside as his horse trotted along, searching for the flower his youngest daughter had assured him he would recognise. He slowed his horse down to a walk but still he could not see a flower which was sufficiently different from any other of its species for him to feel it was the right one for him to pick, the one which would please her most.

The sun had nearly finished its downward journey across the sky when he realized he would not be able to reach home that evening. He urged his horse on in the growing darkness, hoping to reach the home of a friend before he could no longer see the way, and where he could spend the night.

Clouds covered the moon and stars and it was not long after the sun had set that the evening became very dark indeed.

Suddenly he saw a light ahead of him. He urged his horse towards it, feeling sure it was a lamp burning in his friend's house.

But when he arrived at the light he saw it was in the entrance of a stable, a stable that was strange to him. There were no horses stabled there, but there was a great pile of untouched fodder.

He called out a greeting several times, but his voice echoed back and there was no reply. So he unsaddled, watered and fed his horse, carefully hanging up his saddlebags, and resolved to leave money in payment in the morning if he could not find his unknown and unseen host.

The lamp at the entrance of the stable gave off enough light for him to see into each of the empty loose boxes and so he walked the length of the stable, looking into them and wondering in which he would sleep himself. He had put his horse in the loose box opposite the stable door.

Then he saw an open door with a light beyond it at the furthest end of the stable. This he had not noticed before and he hurried towards it, calling out a greeting but, again, there was no reply.

The room he went into was completely empty, except for a chair, a table laid for one person only and with food upon it, hot and ready for eating. And there was an earthenware carafe of cold water, too, and the man drank from it for, by this time, he was very thirsty. He ate all the food and resolved, as he had done in the stable, that if he could find no one about in the strange and silent place the next day, he would leave enough money behind to pay for that which he and his horse had eaten.

He was wondering in which part of the bare room he would sleep or whether it would be better to go back to the stable and sleep in a loose box when he saw another open door which had a light behind it. He could not believe that for a second time he had not noticed an open door and was convinced that it had not been there before. Again he called out, and again there was no reply. And again he went through a doorway which had suddenly appeared.

The room he entered was bare, as the other one had been, except for a bed, freshly made up and ready for use, and a chair. The merchant did that which seemed intended he should: he undressed, put his clothes on the chair and got into bed.

He fell into a dreamless and deep sleep immediately.

The first thing he noticed when he woke up in the morning was that his clothes were no longer on the chair where he had put them when he went to bed. In their place was a brand new set of clothes and a new pair of riding boots. The door was open, as he had left it the previous evening and he had heard nothing during the night.

It was all very strange.

There was nothing else to do but put on the new clothes. They fitted him perfectly, even the boots.

Then he went into the room where he had eaten the night before. The table in the bare room was once again set for one person, the chair was drawn up to the table and, as the man half anticipated in that strange, silent and magical house, breakfast was on the table. The coffee was hot and steaming and yet he had heard no one go into the room, even though the door between the two was still ajar while he dressed.

He ate the meal and went into the stable. All was as it had been the night before except that the lamp over the entrance was no longer alight. Then, for the first time since the merchant had arrived, he felt the cold and prickly sensation of fear: his horse was not in the loose box where he had left it, and the saddlebags containing the red dress and the yellow dress had disappeared.

Quickly he went out into the sunshine and there, peacefully flicking his tail and whisking away a few early morning flies, was his horse. Its reins were attached to a hitching post and it was saddled, the bags holding the dresses the merchant had so carefully chosen for his daughters were in position. He could see at once his presents had not been removed, the fastenings on the saddlebags were as he had left them. His fear fell away from him.

"Is there no one at home?" he called. The horse moved

nervously at the sudden sound. Otherwise there was no reply.

He called out again and again but there was no answer. He decided that before leaving a sum of money (he planned to put it on the table at which he had eaten the two meals, to pay for the lodging for himself and his horse) he would walk around the house and stable and look for his silent host or hostess.

He had barely set off in the direction of the house, when he saw a blaze of colour, just beyond the stable. Never in his life had he seen so many flowers massed together and in such a profusion of hues. When he got closer he saw they were all flowers he had not seen before: there were no cactus flowers or bouganvillea or poinsettias or lilies, the blooms with which he had always been familiar. These flowers had a transparency about them which made them look unlike ordinary flowers: it was as though they had been fashioned from a rainbow.

They were real flowers, but shaped differently from any known species. There were so many of them that it was hard for the man to be sure, but as he gazed at them, marvelling at their beauty and breathing in the sweet scent which seemed to rise from them like a silver vapour shot with gold, he realized that each individual flower had a unique beauty, and that each was different from the rest.

And as he looked at the exquisitely coloured glory spread out before him, the present his youngest daughter had asked for came into his mind. He looked down and there, at his feet, was the flower he knew, as his daughter had told him he would know, which would please her most.

It consisted of a single petal, white with a blush of the palest mauve and it was tubular in shape, but spiralled. It shimmered in the sunshine as though it were filled with crystal, and it was the size of a turkey's egg.

The merchant stooped and picked the flower.

At once it withered between his fingers and, as he watched, it diminished until all that was left of it was a little moisture in the palm of his hand.

For the second time he felt the cold and prickly sensation of fear.

"Do not move," said a harsh male voice.

The merchant turned and saw a beastly creature, a creature unlike any other. It was partly human in that it had arms and legs, but instead of hands and feet it had the scaled claws of a parrot. Its body was covered in curly grey fur. Its

face was human, but of great hideousness and long lank brown hair covered its head, concealing its ears and forehead. The straight hair also grew over its cheeks and chin and thus its mouth could not be seen. The combination of curly grey fur on its body and straight whispy brown air on its head and face was horrible, indeed, to look at. The creature's nose was distended by the unnatural size of its nostrils and its eyes flashed as though they were illuminated from inside the creature's head.

The beastly creature spoke again. "You have accepted my hospitality, put on the new clothes I gave you, eaten my food and allowed your horse to do the same; and then you attempted to steal my beautiful flower. I shall eat you, and eat you alive, for that act of ingratitude."

The merchant begged for his life. He pleaded and implored to be allowed to return to his daughters and he tried to put money into the creature's clawlike hands, in payment for all that he had received.

But the offer was refused.

Then the distraught man said he had not tried to steal the flower for himself but for his youngest daughter. And the monster demanded an explanation.

It made no sound while the man told it of the presents his daughters had asked him to bring them, but it grunted and closed its eyes while the man spoke of how his youngest daughter had told him he would know which flower would please her most and how he had known which one it was.

The creature opened its eyes and said: "You have persuaded me, by telling me of your youngest daughter, that your abuse of my hospitality was unintentional and you may return to your daughters."

The man began expressing his gratitude, but the creature

said: "Be silent and let me finish. You may return to your daughters for three days only. On the third day you will bring your youngest daughter to me and leave her here."

"For how long do you wish my child to stay with you?"

"That is for me to decide, and perhaps your daughter herself will aid me in my decision. If you do not bring her to me on the third day I swear to you that with the monstrous and magical powers which are mine I shall search for you, I shall find you and then I shall eat you. Alive."

The man could think of nothing to say, for he knew he could not bargain with the beastly creature and its magical powers.

"Go now, and remember my instructions must be obeyed if you wish to live into old age. And, furthermore, you shall not take a flower for your youngest daughter. That she shall choose and pluck for herself."

And so the merchant walked back slowly to his horse. When he looked back towards the place where the flowers had been, both they and the beastly creature had vanished.

The cold and prickly sensation of fear came upon him with increasing intensity and he quickly mounted and urged his horse into a gallop.

His fear had subsided by the time he reached home, and the loving welcome his daughters gave him and the pleasure of being with them again banished it completely. He forced the memory of the beastly creature from his mind.

But he had to think about it when his eldest daughter laughingly asked him whether he had perhaps not brought them gifts from the city.

"Indeed I have returned with presents. Go and fetch my saddlebags. I left them in the stable."

The two elder girls were delighted with their dresses. They

fitted perfectly and the eldest looked as beautiful in her flaming red dress as the younger did in her yellow one.

"And, dear Father, did you find and pick the flower you knew would please me most?"

He then had to tell the girls the whole story of his overnight stay in the silent house of the beastly and monstrous creature and, when he reached the end and spoke of the threat the monster had made, the cold and prickly sensation of fear came upon him again, and upon his elder daughters.

But the youngest was not in the least afraid.

"The creature will not try and find you and eat you alive for I shall go to him. I want to see the house in which he lives so silently; and I want to see the magical flowers in his garden even more."

The man was terrified of taking his daughter to the silent place, but he was more fearful for his own life, for the monster had not threatened to harm her at all.

The youngest girl continued to have no trepidation about going and on the third day she urged her father to take her and, to encourage him, she said that if the beastly creature did eat him he would surely eat her too and they would die together. But this did not encourage him at all and he begged her to stay at home with him and her sisters.

"No, we shall go together to the silent place."

The cold and prickly sensation of fear was upon the man as, on the third day after his return home, they saddled their horses and set off, and it remained with him until they reached the place after darkness had fallen. When he saw the lamp at the stable entrance his fear suddenly left him. All was as it had been on his first visit: food and water for the horses, a meal waiting in the room beyond, but this time there were two chairs at the table which had been set with two places. There were two open doors in the room instead of one, each leading into a room with a bed and a chair in it.

And so the merchant and his daughter spent several days there in luxury and idleness, hearing no sound except that of their own voices. Each day new clothes were on the chairs in their rooms and each day meals appeared for them. They searched for the garden of magical flowers but it had disappeared and the man could only try and describe it to his daughter. They did not see the beastly creature at all.

His fear gone, the man decided to return to his home and, for reasons which he could not understand and which she did not understand herself, his daughter refused to go with him.

"Perhaps I shall find the garden with the magical flowers if I am alone here," was all she could say in explanation. She loved her father as he loved her, but go home with him she would not.

It was lonely for the girl in that silent place, but she was content to be there by herself. She had new clothes each morning and each dress she found on the chair when she awoke delighted her more than the ones which had disappeared during the previous night. Her only lack was her inability to find the garden of magical flowers. Eventually she began to miss her family.

After a period of some days she thought it would be pleasant to see them again, on a visit, and she resolved to ride home the following morning. When she awoke she saw a letter lying on top of yet another set of new clothes on the chair by her bed.

The writing was unfamiliar to her. The letter said that there was a little stick on her pillow. She glanced down and there it was: she was sure it had not been there before. She read on. The writer of the letter told her that if she bit the little stick she would find herself with her family. On the third day of her stay she was to bite the stick again and it would bring her back. The letter made no mention of the silent and strange place where she was staying but she knew in her heart that it was to be her new home.

The letter was unsigned but the writer said that if she did not return in three days he, her unseen host, would die.

The young woman did not doubt the truth of all that was written in the letter. She put on her new clothes and then bit on the little stick and immediately found herself upon her horse outside her father's house.

Her family were overjoyed to see her and they spent three happy days together. They could not understand her contentment at the silent place, and even though she had neither seen nor heard the beastly creature and had never been afraid of it they implored her not to return. The girl, who had never before kept any secrets from her family, did not tell them of the letter and its contents: they had no idea it was the little stick which she kept hidden in her bodice that had brought her home and not her horse.

"Even though you have new clothes every day and never have to cook a meal surely it would be happier for you to stay here with us," said one sister.

"And search for a garden you'll never find," continued the other.

The merchant felt the cold and prickly sensation of fear for he had a forboding his youngest daughter would return to the silent place.

On the third day her father and sisters were with her all the time, pleading with her not to leave them, for she had said that that was the day on which she would go back to the silent place. Not until after dark was she able to slip away from them into her old bedroom. There she took the little stick from her dress and bit on it.

At once she was mounted on her horse outside the stable of the silent place. The lamp at the entrance was lit and she dismounted and led her horse inside.

For the first time since she had heard her father's story of his visit to the home of the beastly creature she felt the cold and prickly sensation of fear. But it was not for herself that she was fearful.

She hurried through the stable to the room beyond and there, as usual, was a meal awaiting her. But stretched out on the floor was the monster her father had described. It was dead.

Her fear left her and her only feeling was one of intense sorrow, a grief which was complete and total. To her the beastly creature was not a hideous or fearsome monstrosity: it was the corpse of something or someone which had died alone and unloved. She cradled its hairy head and wept for its loneliness.

After several hours she fell asleep on the floor beside the corpse. She dreamed it was alive again and that it spoke to her, saying: "Go and pick the flower which pleases you most and pour the liquid from its heart onto my head."

She was still weeping when she woke up; and she saw the creature was dead indeed and not alive as in her dream and she lay there crying until there were no more tears to come.

She remembered the dream and wondered about it as she wandered through the stable out into the sunshine.

In front of her she saw a blazing mass of colour. Here at last was the garden of magical flowers of which her father had spoken. She walked towards it and marvelled at the beauty of the flowers, each one different and unlike any other. She looked at them in the mass and tried to look at each one separately, but there were too many and her eyes were dazzled and her mind was bemused by the perfumed vapour which rose from the coloured glory in front of her.

And then she saw by her foot one flower which seemed to excel in loveliness. It was white, faintly tinged with mauve, a spiral single petal and hollow, and it shimmered with a translucent glow. It was the flower which pleased her most.

She plucked it and held it to her face and it was cool against her cheek. Her dizziness left her and she saw there was liquid inside the flower and the memory of her dream flooded back.

Quickly she returned to the corpse and poured the contents of the flower which pleased her most on to its shaggy head.

The beastly creature jerked convulsively and got up. But it was not the monster standing there. In its place stood a handsome and kindly looking young man.

He held out his arms to the girl and took her hands in his and he kissed first the flower and then her hands.

"At last, my love, at last," he whispered.

And she kissed the flower and his hands and answered him.

"At last, my love, at last."

And they held the flower together in their cupped hands and smiled at each other and murmured: "The flower which pleases us both the most."

The New People
and Their Food

THE creation of the world took many centuries to complete (and there are some who say it is not complete yet). In Mexico it is told that not only the formation of the lakes and the mountains and the deserts took place in stages, but that the creation of men and women was a long and difficult process. Some attempts by the gods to populate the earth failed. Others succeeded, but not very well and not for very long.

However, the time did come when there were a few men and a few women and a very few children. But all the work the gods had done in creating them was about to be frustrated yet again: the new people did not know how and what to eat. Without food they would have died and the gods would have had to start all over again and create another race of men and women.

In this particular part of the long saga telling of the continual efforts of the gods to populate the then fairly new world there was one god most immediately concerned. He was Quetzalcoatl. There were other gods involved but he was, if not the greatest, certainly the most effective among the gods in the matter of feeding the new people and keeping them alive. They did not know what was the matter with them, for they had never eaten, but they were very hungry indeed.

It so happened that the ants, which the gods had created long before they had managed to make the new people, not only knew where there was food, but they were able to carry it. The ants did not wish the few new people to die for they felt that if the human race survived it could be made of use to the ant population of the world. So they carried food in their little jaws to the place called Tamoanchan at the time when the men and the women and the children were starving and very weak and approaching the end of their very short lives.

Tamoanchan is the place, the secret place not known to men, where the gods congregate when they have much to do. It was in Tamoanchan that the gods devised their methods of making men and women and it was in Tamoanchan that they met again to decide together how best to keep the people they made alive, this new and very hungry people.

Not a single man and not a single woman and not a single child saw the food which the ants, both black and red, carried into Tamoanchan and to this day no one knows the form the food took. It was not heavy, for a particle of it could be carried by an ant. And that is all that is known. But perhaps it was very hard, because the gods themselves chewed it until it became very soft and moist. The gods did not eat it themselves. They placed it on the lips of the new and starving people, and the people licked it and swallowed it and were satisfied. And for a space their hunger left them.

And the red ants and the black ants again took the food no

man had seen to Tamoanchan and again the gods chewed it so it became very soft and put it on the lips of the new people. This happened again and again, but the god who was Quetzalcoatl knew it could not last. Even he, who loved the new people, grew tired of chewing the food brought by the ants and putting it on the lips of the new people, even though there were very few men and women and fewer children.

Quetzalcoatl understood that the other gods would not feed the human race indefinitely, for the gods had other things to do, such as arranging for the rain to fall and the rivers to flow and the waves to rise upon the oceans. A people who could not keep alive by feeding themselves were a people not worthy of the gods who had given them life. This Quetzalcoatl, and only Quetzalcoatl, knew and understood. He wished to make the new people worthy of their gods and creators.

Whether the ants told him or whether it was something the god, Quetzalcoatl, was simply aware of is not known. But it is known that Quetzalcoatl was conscious of the fact that underneath a massive mountain grains of corn were hidden, grains which could be eaten by the new people and planted by them too. And Quetzalcoatl knew also that the grains which the new people could be taught to plant would grow and multiply into a never ending supply.

Perhaps the other gods knew these things too. But they did not care enough for the new people to find the corn and Quetzalcoatl realized that very soon they would not even care to chew the edible substance brought by the ants to feed the new people, and so keep them alive.

The ants knew the way into the secret place in the mountain as they knew the way to the secret and holy place called Tamoanchan, but they would not reveal where the corn was

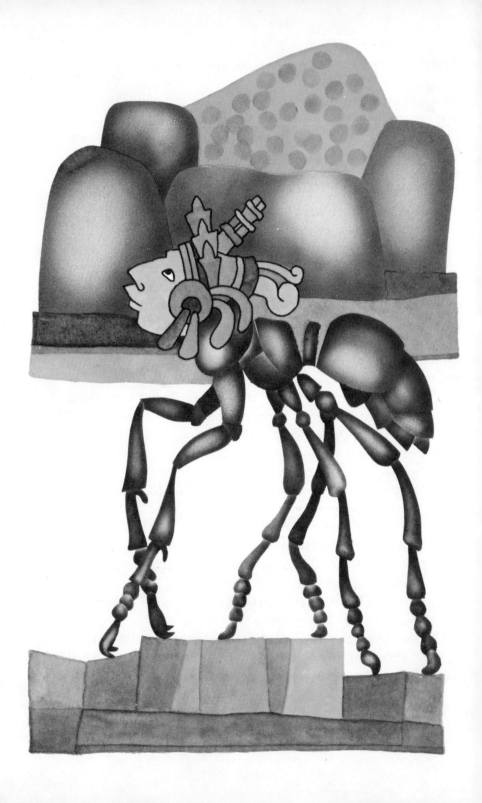

hidden, not even to the god Quetzalcoatl. Perhaps this was because they enjoyed their self imposed task of going to Tamoanchan, the meeting place of the gods. Or perhaps they thought the gods would favour them if they continued to help keep the new people alive rather than enable them to feed themselves. Possibly the ants really just wanted to keep the human race in permanent subjugation.

But Quetzalcoatl was not to be thwarted by the obstinacy or selfishness of any ant and he turned himself into one. He chose to be a black ant.

None of the ants, neither black nor red, knew that he had become one of them. It was not very long before he joined in one of their processions, moving in the way ants do, one after the other, into the very centre of the great mountain. And there was the granary of life-giving corn, never seen by man and only then by one god, the good god, Quetzalcoatl.

The god was not strong enough to open the mountain alone and give the corn to the new people. So Quetzalcoatl returned to Tamoanchan with the ant procession and there told the gods of the corn which is food for men and women and children.

The god who is Thunderbolt split the mountain open with a single blow and Quetzalcoatl shed his guise of a black ant and himself gave the grains of corn to the new people. And he and Thunderbolt saw they were able to chew and eat it without help.

And all the gods were glad that Quetzalcoatl had discovered corn and that he, with Thunderbolt, had given it to the new people, who now knew how to keep themselves alive.

Only the Rain God, Tlaloc, was jealous of the power of self preservation given to the new people. He stole the corn they had not already eaten, and it is in his possession still.

But the people, who are no longer new, can still eat. For Quetzalcoatl told their forebears how and where to plant the grains of corn and Tlaloc, who had taken it for his own, watered it and waters it still and it grows and multiplies.

When the new people planted the grains of corn, plants grew but there were only two seeds upon each of them. Gradually Tlaloc, with his rain, increased the size of the corn plants and gave them cobs to bear the grains. Now the plants have several cobs and they carry many grains and the grains themselves are much, much bigger than the first ones Quetzalcoatl found in the mountain.

And where there is corn which has been planted by the people who are no longer new, and when the Rain God Tlaloc works for his stolen possession, no man nor woman nor child has been hungry since Quetzalcoatl followed the ants into the mountain which held food which was vital to the new people then and to all people now.

The Brothers and the Singing Toad

THERE was once a farmer in Yucatan. His farm was large, some miles from the inland town of Merida. He was not very rich and not very poor and he considered himself lucky. His maize crops were always excellent and his three sons helped him in his fields.

When he was no longer young, but before he was old, he began to think that he might become very rich, so bountiful were the harvests and so hard working were his three sons, particularly the youngest one.

The middle aged man and the three young men were satisfied with their life together, but the father wished for at least one of his sons to marry. His wife had died soon after their youngest son was born and he knew that there could be no true contentment on the farm without a woman there too. The elder sons were too busy helping their father to get very rich (and thus rich themselves) to bother about finding wives. Only the youngest sometimes wished he had a wife as beautiful and kind as he had been told his mother, whom he could not remember, had been.

By the time the farmer was on the verge of becoming old he had become very rich indeed and, while this pleased him, he was not yet fully content for not one of those four men on the farm had a wife.

One morning when the farmer and his sons went to start harvesting the ripe maize cobs they found, to their horror, that about a tenth of the largest field had been ravaged. They could tell the destruction had not been caused by a man or men. It was definitely the work of an animal. They searched the area for tracks but found none.

The following morning more of the maize plants had been uprooted and the cobs stripped of their yield.

This continued, night after night, until there was less than half of the maize left in the field to harvest.

The farmer and his sons had reaped the rest of their fields, but the father feared for his farm and his fortune. Until the unknown creature which at night systematically destroyed the crop in his largest field had been found great wealth could no longer be his.

So he summoned his sons and said he would leave all his money to whichever one killed or captured the animal and that he would leave his farm to the son who married first.

Of the three young men it was the youngest who loved the farm the best, but where, he wondered, could he find a wife who was both beautiful and kind?

His elder brothers cared more for riches than farm work.

Because the youngest brother was eager to help his father and because the other two were eager to be assured of his fortune for the time when they too were no longer young, all three volunteered to go and find the beast that very night.

The farmer insisted that each son should try and kill or capture the creature alone. The two elder sons each begged to be allowed to go that evening and the third son suggested they should all go together. Their father was adamant and said they should each, in order of age, try to rid the field of its nightly marauder. He told his eldest son he might go that night.

The second son feared their father's fortune would not be his and the third son feared lest none of them could find the creature and that their father's old age would be unhappy because of their failure.

So the eldest son set off for the field with a gun, a piece of baked maize dough in case he became hungry during the night, and a great deal of confidence.

Near the field there was a well and the young man proposed to watch for the animal there. But seated beside the well was a toad, singing.

The youth told it to be quiet. But it sang more loudly. Then the youth shouted at it to stop. Still the toad sang and sang.

"Stop that terrible singing. I am waiting for the creature who steals my father's maize and the noise you make will frighten the most savage of beasts."

"I know why you are here and I tell you the thief does not come this way," answered the singing and talking toad, "and, furthermore, it likes my songs."

And it began to sing again.

"Nonsense, neither man nor beast could like the noise you are making."

"Then take me to the maize field and I will prove it to you. I will show you the stealer of your father's corn and you shall hear me sing to it."

"You are an absurd and lying reptile with an untuneful voice."

Having said that the young man lost his temper and picked up the toad and threw it down the well.

Even though he did not believe what the singing toad had said about the thief liking its voice, he did think that perhaps it would not pass that way, so he went straight to the field to watch for it there.

All night long he waited but nothing came that he could see or hear. It was very quiet in the field and even the toad in the well was silent.

In the early dawn the young man saw that the thief had visited the field during the hours of darkness, for several plants had been stripped of their cobs.

Chewing on his hunk of maize dough, he stumped off to his home in a thoroughly bad mood. He sulkily admitted to his father and brothers that he had seen and heard nothing in the field except the results of the pillaging which had occurred during the night. He did not mention his encounter with the singing toad.

And so the second son went off that day long before it became dark to keep his vigil for the beast none of them had seen. As his brother had done he took with him a gun, some baked maize dough and even more confidence than the eldest son. He, too, stopped by the well and was exceedingly rude to the toad who was singing there.

The toad stopped his song and said: "I shall not keep quiet. I like singing."

"Your voice has no tunefulness at all and the noise will drive away the creature which steals my father's maize from the field over there. Be quiet! I am here to kill the beast, and if you go on singing I shall kill you too."

The toad sang a short song very loudly and then said: "I will help you find the creature who pays nightly visits to the field, but stop singing my songs I will not."

"You could not help me stalk the beast. Only by stopping that terrible noise could you be of any use to me."

"If you give me some of your maize dough cake I might stop singing for a little while."

The second son of the farmer immediately threw the maize cake away. The toad, who disliked the young man as much as he had disliked his elder brother, bounded to where it had fallen, ate it all up and, leaping back to the side of the well, began singing again.

This made the farmer's son even more furious and he picked up the toad by its foot and flung it down the well.

Then he went to the field.

As his brother had done before him, he waited all night but saw and heard nothing. But he did see, in the morning, that more maize plants had been spoiled. Although disconsolate and disgruntled, he returned at once to his father and brothers and told them he had failed in his task. But he did not mention the toad.

So the third and youngest brother set off with a maize dough cake and a gun. Instead of confidence he went on his mission with trepidation. He wondered how he could possibly succeed where both his brothers had failed.

As he approached the well he heard the toad singing.

"That is a very fine song sung with a very fine voice," he said when the toad had finished.

"And that is the first courteous remark I have heard from any of your family."

"Oh, do you know them?"

"Only your brothers. I have not met your father."

"You must meet him. He would like your singing too."

The toad did not answer or say how he had met the elder brothers. He just puffed himself up and sang another longer and louder song.

The third son again complimented the toad, saying: "I think that is an even finer song than the one you sang before."

"Yes, it is. But I can sing still finer songs than that. Later you may hear all the songs I know, but now I am going to help you."

"Can it be you know why I am here?"

"Indeed, I know, but I shall not tell you how I know. Will you take me to the field?"

"Of course I will. And will you sing to me there?"

"I shall decide that later," the toad replied. "Now, before we go I must tell you something. There is a magic stone, it is an emerald actually, lying at the bottom of the well. Only I have ever seen it. It can and does grant wishes. So, what is your wish?"

112

"There are many things I wish to have."

"Well, the magic emerald will grant you more than one wish. Only do not make the list too long, we must be off to the maize field soon."

"Can the magic emerald really grant *anything*?"

"Yes, I said so."

"Or someone?"

"What do you mean?"

"A wife, for instance?"

"Of course, but you had better tell the stone the sort of wife you want. A good cook, perhaps? And that reminds me. I am hungry. Please, may I have a piece of your maize dough cake?"

The third son gave the toad the whole cake. When the toad had eaten he sang a little song of pleasure.

"Now, young man, wish. Lean over the well so the stone may hear you clearly. And you had better wish for a house so you can give your wife a home."

And so the young man wished for a wife who would be both beautiful and kind, a fine house near the well so that he and his bride could live near the singing toad; and he did not forget to wish for success in finding the marauder of the maize field.

"We must be off," said the toad.

They went to the field. It was only early afternoon and darkness was several hours away. The toad sang from the young man's shoulder where he had put it to carry it and the young man wondered, as he walked, how soon his wishes would be granted.

They had barely settled themselves down at the edge of the field when the young man saw an enormous white bird hovering above them. It was of a species he had never seen

before. Suddenly it swooped down and began tearing cobs off the maize plants with its heavy curved bill, then clawing up the plants with its hooked feet.

The young man raised his gun and took aim.

"Do not shoot," cried the toad, and promptly began to sing.

The bird stopped stripping the maize and flew across the field and settled down beside the toad, fluffing out its feathers. The toad sang and sang and the bird cooed with pleasure. The young man was thoroughly amazed. The toad sang a lullaby and the bird went to sleep. The young man stroked its feathered head and thought it very beautiful.

"How can such a lovely creature as this destroy our crop and give my father such distress?"

"It cannot help it. I will explain."

And then the toad told the young man that the bird was

really a beautiful maiden who had been turned into a maize marauding bird by a witch.

"But why should the witch do that?"

"Because she is evil and because she has an equally evil son whom the maiden refused to marry. It was the witch's revenge on the girl for slighting her son. The bird just cannot help stealing maize. I it was who caused it always to come to this field, for I knew all about you (and how I knew I shall not say) and now, helped by the magic emerald, my plan is nearly complete."

The toad then broke into a song of happiness.

After the beautiful white bird had woken up they all went to the young man's home, he carrying the bird all the way, for it was drowsy, and he also feared it might fly away even though the toad assured him it would not.

"It is your bird now," the toad said.

The young man showed the bird to his father and brothers and said it was the creature for which they had all searched. The toad sang a song which the farmer greatly enjoyed and at which the elder brothers scoffed.

Then the elder brothers tried to take the bird from the young man's arms. He held it firmly but suddenly it flew from his grasp and he ran after it, the toad leaping along in pursuit.

The bird flew in the direction of the large maize field and then disappeared.

When the young man reached the well he saw there was a fine house standing between it and the field. A young woman came out, her hands outstretched towards him. He saw she was beautiful and he knew at once she was kind. She gave him a single white feather as proof that she had been the bird.

The toad hopped about in excitement and said: "Come on, young man, it is up to you now to make your first wish come true."

So the young man asked the young woman to marry him and she said she would. And then the three of them returned to the farmer.

The farmer said he would leave his fortune and his farm to his youngest son and this he did. In due time, when he died, the youngest son and his wife and their children were very rich indeed, with a very prosperous farm. But before all that happened, and soon after the youngest son had married the kind and beautiful young woman, the elder brothers went away to Merida.

The farmer stayed in his home until he became very old and then he went to live with his son and daughter-in-law in the fine house by the well. And all the while the youngest son cared for the farm while his wife cared for him, their children and her father-in-law.

And the toad sang and sang.

They never knew whether the elder brothers became very rich in the town, for they never came back and they utterly neglected their father in his old age.

The farmer was truly content. His maize field was no longer ravaged and there was a woman in his family. The singing toad sang to them all and they loved him for it.

So happy were they all that the toad never had to remind the young man of the magic emerald at the bottom of the well which would have granted him any wish he might have had for himself or his wife or his father or, later on, his children.

The young man, who had proved himself to be as kind as the beautiful wife he had wished for, wanted for nothing else except, perhaps, for the toad to sing him more new songs. But the toad sang them anyway.

Tepoztecatl

SOME say that Tepoztecatl was a god, one of four hundred who looked after the agriculture in and around the village of Tepoztlan. Others say he was a god of drunkeness and that he was hideous to look at. But perhaps those who say that are jealous of him, for there is much about Tepoztecatl which men might envy. He was certainly a hero and like all true heroes he had qualities which no ordinary mortals have, and some of these qualities were magical.

In the days when Tepoztecatl lived in Tepoztlan, during his manhood, he was able to make rain come when a drought threatened. But no one knew how he did it. And when the village was surrounded by enemies, all prepared to descend the cliffs and hills which encircle it, he dispersed them, single handed. It is not known how he did that, either. He also helped a goddess called Mayahuel turn the juice of maguey plants into beer, but no one knew exactly how that was done. Perhaps because he had helped make the first beer in Mexico, *pulque* is its name, some people say he was a god of drunkeness. But Tepoztecatl was always heroic in his manner and the deeds he performed were never done when he was drunk. He could not have done them if he had been.

There are other tales about Tepoztecatl, when he was a man and when he was a boy, and there are different stories, too, about him when he was a baby.

Some say a princess found a little clay doll by the river where she was bathing and that when she picked it up it

118

turned into a baby, who was Tepoztecatl. It is also told that he was found by three princesses on an antheap. This was magical also, for instead of biting the infant the ants had covered his naked body with tiny flowers to protect him from the sun and had fed the child with honey. The three princesses watched the baby for a little while and then left him in the care of the ants, for he was a healthy looking baby, and happy too, and they felt that this was not an abandoned child as he had countless ants to tend him.

Then there are some who say that Tepoztecatl was abandoned by his mother, but no one knows who she was unless she was the princess who picked up the clay doll by the river. Those who say this about him tell of his being found by an old couple as a baby of only a few days old. They found him in a box, floating down the river. If it was the same river as the one by which the clay doll was found, perhaps that is the true story of his birth.

There are even people who believe that Tepoztecatl came out of a chicken's egg and that, for the first few days of his life, he was the size of a baby chicken. And these people say that, although he never grew bigger than a fully grown hen, he had extraordinary strength and intelligence and was able, when only two months old, to play the guitar. And the guitar he played was not a tiny one to suit his diminutive size, but one made for a man. When Tepoztecatl played upon it the melodies were beautiful and haunting and no one but the tiny little baby could play them. But now that Tepoztecatl has gone, no one remembers the tunes he played, if play them he really did.

While the story of Tepoztecatl has so many beginnings a story from his childhood varies not at all.

However or wherever he was born, he had no known

parents. He did, however, have grandparents. They were not really his grandparents, but he thought of them as such and they brought him up as though he was their grandson. They had no other child but Tepoztecatl.

The old couple loved the child very much and they were proud of him, too. He was not like other children, for he displayed his heroic qualities very early in life. He never grew very tall, but he had a strength which is not given to other boys and his intelligence was greater than that of the wisest of men.

Before he was two years of age he taught himself to make a bow. The old couple watched, amazed, as he bent a long stick, as thick as one of his own arms, and tied the two ends tightly with a string he had made from twisted fibres of the maguey plant. Little Tepoztecatl had never seen the old man use a bow, and certainly had not seen him make one, but he made his as though he was a man long experienced in its making and its use. After he had tested the tautness of the maguey fibre string with his little fingers, he put the new bow down and trotted off down the path towards the cliffs.

His grandparents were speechless with astonishment at what he had done.

Soon he came back to them, carrying some sticks and pieces of obsidian which he had picked up. He settled down on the ground beside his bow and, watched by the odd couple, proceeded to peel the bark off the sticks and then, with strong deft movements, he broke them into equal lengths. The couple did not ask the baby boy what he was doing, for it was obvious. They just watched him chip and notch the pieces of obsidian into arrowheads and then bind them firmly to one end of each stick, using the fibre twine left over from the bow.

Then the baby announced calmly in a very grown-up

voice that he was going to hunt for their supper. But he stayed where he was for, as he said this, a bird flew over, a brilliantly coloured macaw, and Tepoztecatl picked up his bow and one of his arrows and took aim at the bird circling above him and shot the arrow from the bow. The macaw fluttered and dropped at the feet of the old man.

It was the first time the little child had even tried to shoot. After that he always provided food for his grandparents and himself; rabbits and birds and deer. And he helped them grow vegetables, tomatoes and sweet peppers, too, and corn. All through his boyhood he looked after his grandparents by feeding his little family, and they looked after him by giving him a home.

Although he was always small and never grew very tall in the way some heroes do, it is said that he had the strength of a giant by the time he was eight. He was clever, too, at making things; curved sticks with which to till the soil and blow-pipes for hunting. And he made sandals for the old couple as well as for himself, but he liked making bows and arrows best and he had a large collection of these.

All went very happily in the village of Tepoztlan for the grandparents and for Tepoztecatl throughout his childhood. But when he was still a boy, verging on manhood, the great giant Xochicalcatl announced, through his retainers, that he intended his next meals to come from Tepoztlan.

Xochicalcatl's warriors came into the village to spread this news. They harmed no one, but the people were much afraid for they knew that the meals Xochicalcatl ate had caused much sorrow and suffering in the surrounding villages. The great giant only ate old men. He neve touched animal flesh, or birds or fish. He never ate young men or women, and he had never been known to eat a child.

The warriors of Xochicalcatl told Tepoztecatl's grandfather that he was to be the first of the meals the giant would have from Tepoztlan.

"You are well fed," they said, "for we know your grandson provides you and your wife with more than enough to eat. You will make an excellent meal from Tepoztlan for Xochicalcatl."

And they told him they would come back within five days to fetch him and that he was to eat well and fatten himself up in the meantime.

Then the giant's warriors left the village.

The old man and the old woman were greatly afraid. Tepoztecatl, however, showed no fear at all. He said he would take his grandfather's place and be eaten instead by Xochicalcatl.

"But, my grandson, Xochicalcatl never eats children. We have never heard of him doing that."

"I am nearly a man now, and I promise you he will eat me instead of you."

"But why should you die instead of me? I am old and you are young. It is more fitting that Xochicalcatl should eat me."

"Grandfather, I assure you that I will not die when Xochicalcatl eats me."

"How can that be? No one has ever been able to escape from Xochicalcatl's stomach."

"I shall, I promise you."

"Can you prove this to your grandmother and to me?"

"I shall try."

Tepoztecatl left his grandparents then and went walking in the hills around Tepoztlan. There was one a little higher than the others, called Cuicuizacatlan. The boy stood at its foot for a long time, and what he thought about no one knows. But

when he began walking again instead of going up Cuicuiza-catlan he walked right through it. Then he turned round and walked through the hill again. And then he went back to his grandparents.

"I have proved that I can escape from Xochicalcatl's stomach," he said.

"How?" they asked.

"I have just walked through Cuicuizacatlan. I have walked through twice."

His grandparents believed him and did not ask him how he had done it. They remembered that, as a baby, he had made a bow, and arrows too, without having been taught how or told what they were for, and that he had used that bow to shoot a macaw without having practised with it at all. So they thought it not strange that in his boyhood he should have walked through Cuicuizacatlan and back again.

When Xochicalcatl's warriors returned to Tepoztlan they could not find the old man. The old woman had disappeared too. Only Tepoztecatl was there. He told the troops his grandparents had gone away and that he would not tell them where they were. The warriors did not try to find the old couple for they could tell from the way the boy spoke that indeed he would not say anything more about his grand-parents and that they had gone to a place where they would never be found.

"Take me to Xochicalcatl," commanded Tepoztecatl.

"But you are only a boy," the warriors said.

"I am nearly a man. Take me."

And again because of the way Tepoztecatl spoke the warriors knew that take him they must.

Tepoztecatl walked with the warriors out of the village and into the hills. He took nothing with him except a little leather bag. The warriors asked him what was in it.

"Only two arrowheads," was the reply.

"What use are arrowheads if you have no arrows?" they asked.

"They are of use to no one. Only to me."

The warriors laughed at him but let him keep the little bag, and after that they asked him no more questions.

It took a long while for the warriors and Tepoztecatl to reach Xochicalco, where the great giant Xochicalcatl lived. They walked for two days and one night and then they were there. On the first day they climbed Cuicuizacatlan and it took them all the morning to reach the top and most of the afternoon to come down the other side. Tepoztecatl smiled all the time they climbed up and down the hill, but he said nothing. The warriors said nothing either, but they did not smile at all.

Xochicalcatl roared when he heard them coming: "I am hungry! I am hungry! Where is the old man?"

And he ordered those who served him to heat the big cauldron of water, for he liked his meals boiled rather than roasted.

When the warriors brought in the youthful Tepoztecatl instead of an old man Xochicalcatl was furious. He kicked over the great pot of boiling water and scalded those who were near it.

"This is a boy, a mere boy! I shall eat him as he is: he may prove to be a tasty morsel, but he is too young and too small to be a meal."

"I am nearly a man," said Tepoztecatl.

But the great giant said nothing to the boy. He dismissed his warriors and charged them to find an old man in his dotage from Tepoztlan, preferably the old man, of whom they had told him, who was so well fed by his grandson.

"This is that old man's grandson," the warriors said. "We believe you will find him very good to eat."

The giant merely roared again and told them to bring the old grandfather to him immediately. But the warriors knew they would never find him, and so they went and hid in the hills. They were never heard of again. Some say they lived out their lives in the hills between Xochicalco and Tepoztlan, while some say they live there still, hiding and never seen.

Xochicalcatl picked up Tepoztecatl and ate him. "Too young for boiling," he grunted as he swallowed him whole.

Directly Tepoztecatl reached the giant's stomach he opened his leather bag and took out the two arrowheads. With one in each hand he began cutting his way out. The obsidian arrowheads were sharp and it took only a little time for Tepoztecatl to step out into the daylight.

It was not difficult for the youth to escape from the giant,

but that escape was most painful for Xochicalcatl. The agony of the walls of his stomach being cut by obsidian arrowheads made him faint, and by the time Tepoztecatl was running back to Tepoztlan the great giant had died of his pain.

Tepoztecatl reached the village far, far more quickly than it had taken him to walk to Xochicalco with the warriors for he ran through, rather than over or around, the hills. But no one saw him do it.

When he arrived his grandparents appeared from their secret hiding place. No one knows, even now, where that place was. They greeted Tepoztecatl most joyfully, but he just reminded them that he had promised he would not die in Xochicalcatl's stomach.

"I am nearly a man," he said.

Perhaps of all the stories told of Tepoztecatl the one which is told most often is how he stopped for all time old men being eaten in their dotage by the great giant of Xochicalco. Perhaps of all the deeds performed by Tepoztecatl that was the most heroic. And yet, because it was so simple for Tepoztecatl to cut his way out of Xochicalcatl's stomach perhaps it was also the least of his heroic deeds. But however easy a task it was, it was worth performing and Tepoztecatl performed it in his boyhood and he performed it well. And it was surely by this single action that he, reputed to be a god and a child of magic, truly proved himself to be a hero.

But all Tepoztecatl had to say about it at the time was: "I am nearly a man."